I0192644

Previous Books and Chapbooks

The Colors of the World

Landscapes

The Well Under the Pawpaw Trees

Moon of Changing Seasons

Dissolving Forms

Liquidambar

The House on Afternoon Street

Sometimes the Light

Stars Scattered Like Seeds

Carrying Water in a Sieve

Meditation for the Earth

Angelus

In a Rose Wood Wandering

At the Horizon Line

Summoning

Summoning

JEANNE SHANNON

Summoning
Copyright ©2016 Jeanne Shannon

ISBN: 978-1-940769-48-6
Publisher: Mercury HeartLink
Printed in the United States of America

Author photo by Julie Dunlop

All rights reserved. This book, or sections of this book,
may not be reproduced or transmitted in any form
without permission from the author.

Permission is granted to educators to create copies of
individual poems for classroom or workshop assignments.

Contact Jeanne Shannon at JSPoetry@aol.com

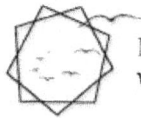

Mercury HeartLink
www.heartlink.com

Thanks to the editors of the journals and anthologies where some of these poems have appeared, including *Adobe Walls, Bitterroot, BlazeVOX, Clinch Mountain Review, Cloudbank, Crab Creek Review, Dalhousie Review, Glint Literary Journal, Grasslimb, Hamilton Stone Review, Indefinite Space, Iodine Poetry Journal, Isotope, Lilliput Review, Lunarosity, Malpais Review, Midway Journal, Moon Milk Review, Petrichor Machine, Poetry from the Other Side* anthology, *Postcard Poems and Prose, Psychic Meatloaf, Shadow and Light* anthology, *Solo Novo, The Blue Hour, The Rag,* and *Tule Review.*

"Neon" contains phrases that are improvisations on lines by Malina Mörling, Morri Creech and Charles H. Webb.

Summoning

ACKNOWLEDGEMENTS

I. DISSOLVING FORMS

3   At the Horizon Line

4   Circles, Dissolving

6   Shimmer

7   Glow

8   From an Item Titled "Best International News," January 1986

9   Candela

10   Alternative News, and Notes from *The Pastel Journal*

12   A Disappearance in Tennessee

14   Dissolving Forms

16   Objects in Mirror Are Closer Than They Appear

18   Imbolc

19   Page From a Book of Hours

20   Easter Morning

21   Counterpoint

22   Arthur Means **Bear** in Brythonic

23   Sycamore

24   Echoes of Water in a Mirror

26   Night in a Town on Boldcamp Mountain

27   Elsewhere

28   All I Know is What I Know

29   Dancing All Night at the Tribulation Café

30   Sulfur

32   City Inside the Blizzard

34   Notes Written in Purple Ink

36   Southern Cross

38   A Little Sweetness in the Noonday Light

41   Interstices

42   Opal

43   Marigold

44   The Town

46   The World Seen Through Broken Glass

48   Notes from the Fractal Cosmos

II. THE COLORS OF THE WORLD

55   Fourteen Ways of Looking at a Painting by Georgia O'Keeffe

58   In the Studio

59   Flower

60   Goosegog, Foxtail, Katydid

62   Canvas

63   Names the Color of Rain

64   Greece

66   In a Pastel City Under the Pleiades

67   Silver

68   The Horse of the Dream

70   Neon

72   Wood Wind

74   Floodlight

76   Angelus

78   The Artist Longs to Emulate Wolf Kahn

79   From a Painting of the Annunciation

80   Les Vergers En Fleur

82   Intense Yellow of a Rising Sun: The Artist Emulates Van Gogh

83   Bank of the Oise at Auvers

84   Landscape With Woman Walking Beside a River

86   K.M.

87   First Day of Spring

88   If I Had a Daughter

90   Advice to the Poet

III. HONEY LOCUST

95   Moon of Popping Trees

96   Meditation for the Earth

98   New Mexico: Days and Nights of Early Spring

99   At Sundown, Bosque del Apache Wildlife Refuge

100   North Valley Spring

101   In the Month of Willow and Blackthorn

102   Early April, Elm Trees Heavy With Chartreuse Flowers

103   In Middle April

104   Last Thursday in April

105   All Day the Wind

106   Beltane

108   June

109   Honey Locust

110   Escape to Taos

112   Jemez Springs, New Mexico

114   Lilac

115   Dark of the Moon

116   Litha

117   Summer Morning

118   Divisions

119   Locust Cry

120   Rain

122   Tickseed Sunflower

123   Hedge Bindweed

124   Midsummer at Gilliam Court

125   Orchard, Grove

126   July Nights

127   August

128   Along the Clinch River at Dungannon, Virginia

129   Dog Days

130   September, and Strawberry Leaves Redden Around the Edges

131   Evensong

132   September Villanelle

133   In the Time of Yellow Leaves

134   Autumn

135   Bach on an Autumn Evening, a Forest in New Mexico

136   Continuous Nuclear Reactions

138   Why I Wrote Out by Hand Ronald Johnson's *The Book of the Green Man* on an Autumn Evening in 1970

141   November Evening, New Mexico

142   Sandia Night

143   Tulip Tree Standing in the North Fork of the Powell River,
          Appalachia, Virginia

144   Solstice

146   December Noon

IV. SUMMONING

151   Geraniums

152   A Season

153   Waiting for Rain

154   Where the Fairground Was in 1948

155   Toward the Blue Rooms of What We Remember

156   Forsythia

158   Florida Coast, 1955

159   Counting the Stars of Ten Thousand Years Ago

160   Shadow

161   San Diego Summer Afternoon, Songs From the Forties Playing

162   Carolina Allspice

163   Summoning

164   Song for Uncle Emerson

165   When Panthers Roamed in the Blue Ridge

168   Songs

173   Meditation in February

174   Cumberland

176   Carrying Water in a Sieve

177   Patterns

178   Hazel Mountain

180   Pavane

183   Autumn, and Lady Day Singing "We May Never Meet Again"

184   Evening

186   In the Bois de Boulogne, August 1914

188   Going Blind in April

189   After That Morning

190   She Had a Farm in Africa

192   Singing the Duende

194   Nocturn

196   For Alice, Saying Goodbye

V. ETUDE: PRIME NUMBERS

200   Etude: Prime Numbers

VI. OF THE HOURS, SEAMLESS

209   Of the Hours, Seamless

       ABOUT THE AUTHOR

For my husband, John,
who entered a brighter world
on the first day of May, 2015

In memory of our fifty-eight years together. . .
and all the summers that have gone like smoke

I. DISSOLVING FORMS

At the Horizon Line

world suffused with mystery and light

shimmer breaks through
the scrim of what seems to be

we tremble
on the cusp of the seen and unseen

shapes change and vanish, reappear:
waves in a white sea

the past with its shadows
its carnival dreams

what is certain?

what is only
the ghost-smoke
of our heart's longing?

CIRCLES, DISSOLVING

The questions are more interesting than the answers.

—Sandra Moore Starr

In a carbon sky
the tireless stars keep wheeling.

Who will cut out paper flowers
and feed a sick cat with a syringe?

Think of honey,
how it carries the souls of flowers,
how it seeps beyond boundaries.

Is it a mirage, this pool of amber?

Whose childhood
is in the patchwork quilt—

a square of yellow-blossomed fabric
from a dress she wore
the summer she was nine?

Where does the mystery begin—
the book of echoes,
notes of lyre and dulcimer?

What do we mean by *now*?
London on a June day in 1923,
Clarissa Dalloway buying flowers?

A clock strikes,
sending its leaden circles
up, up, into the rook-filled air.

The simultaneity of time.

What do we mean by *now*?

SHIMMER

I saw a woman standing in the air
    What will you do if
above St. Cuthbert Street
      you don't have any cloudberries?

and morning was in the light

and sorrow-weed
and hanging gardens

O, come with me to Sumer, Akkad
      What will you do if
      you fall asleep
We will recite the calculus of stars
      and find yourself in Babylon?

It is a sound like purple smoke

GLOW

"She dreams of flying naked through the air
unhindered by all the paraphernalia
of who she is."

> — *Amari Hamadene*
> *from "The Yellow Sparrowhawk"*

All day
we roam
the phenomenal world

> grass   almond tree
> coffee cup   ardor

but
at night
in sleep

elsewhere

> *compass rose   shooting star   topaz*

From an Item Titled "Best International News," January 1986

Six Soviet cosmonauts
said they witnessed
a band of glowing angels
with wings as big
as jumbo jets.

"What we saw from Salyut 7
were seven giant figures
in the form of humans

but with wings
and mistlike haloes."

After many hours
the angels went away,
but twelve days later
they returned.

"They were smiling,"
said Svetlana Savitskaya,

"as though they knew
some glorious secret."

CANDELA

in fact:

spring light
is pouring black tulips from a pitcher

the Virgin:

stands in the walnut tree
cool as a charmed quark

rose trees bow down
it is burning noon

says to me:

behold
gold angels
landing in the cherry leaves

extract
the radium of the word

ALTERNATIVE NEWS, AND NOTES FROM
THE PASTEL JOURNAL

April rainfall near the North Pole.

Sheila Goodman paints the land and aqueous scenery of England's countryside.

"Rain in the High Arctic in April is nothing short of bizarre," said David Phillips, senior climatologist with Environment Canada.

At the border between Hampshire and Dorset.

Yes, honeybees are in terminal decline.

Goodman's "Summer Watermeadow": Yellow trees, abstract in the green mirror of the water.

What will we eat if all the bees die?

An evening meadow stretches away, purple under a lavender sky.

In 1909 in *Popular Mechanics* magazine, Nikola Tesla predicted text messaging.

Using either charcoal or acrylic, Goodman establishes the horizon line and places the main elements.

Through experiments in high-voltage electricity and magnetic fields, Tesla discovered that time and space could be breached, or warped, creating a "doorway" that could lead to other times.

She starts with an area where three tones meet.

Physicists posit the possibility of a parallel Earth in which the Twin Towers are still standing and the Hindenburg never exploded.

Rising sun reflected in a blue river.

In Los Alamos, the fast-food cook making your hamburger may be from another galaxy. Classified ads may be secret messages to beings from other dimensions. Crop circles speak to those who can read the code. The Men In Black are said to be here only as observers. But did they murder the reporter who wrote about West Virginia's Mothman?

Roomscapes. Pastel interiors of Sandra Burshell. Inspiration rooted in the past. Quiet images reminiscent of Degas and Bonnard.

Did Tesla die of natural causes?

A DISAPPEARANCE IN TENNESSEE

September 23, 1880

(For David Lang, wherever he may be)

> *"In full view of three witnesses, on*
> *a flat, treeless, stubble-grass field,*
> *Lang had simply VANISHED."*

1. where he walked
    no
    shadow falls
    no
    cricket cries

    birds
    lose their way
    their compasses
    torn apart by a raging void

2. father
    father
    it was only
    an autumn day
    a field of stubble-grass

    where did you go
    through that winesap air?

3. grapes hung purple
    in leafy arbors

    cattle lay down
    in September grass

the earth was an island
of limestone bedrock
and all of its boundaries
were known

but a chasm opened that afternoon
along moon-white edges
of other worlds

4. in April evenings
    a milk-glass moon
    haunted the pasture
    where he vanished

    his children called to him
    and he replied

    his muffled voice
    cracking the starlit air
    apart

DISSOLVING FORMS

unstable particles

>   charmed quarks
>   hadrons
>   topaz poppies in new bloom

>> *in summer there is a river*
>> *where bees drink in their blue thirst*
>> *but now in January*
>> *only kaleidoscopes*
>> *of cold and wind*

energies

>   gold wool\red silk\the skin of tangerines

>> *the men go south*
>> *to capture memories*
>> *of an exploding star*

>> *(gamma rays falling*
>> *   so purely*
>> *   toward Alice Springs)*

>> *bees swim toward Australia*
>> *in their blue joy*

crystals\mirrors

>   water that swirls in pools
>   the water tower at Charlotte Street
>   rainsilver on Black Lake

a rosary
      where peaches grow
      and briary vines

      (and steep light filters
      through rose quartz)

         at home   the women
         who must write of this
         are turning the pages of old books

         imagining light from supernovae

         thirsting for light from
         the Southern Cross

Objects in Mirror Are Closer Than They Appear

I am finished with my morning song   Distant leaves
beckon   Precise images   slow to a sleepwalk

Scarred angels/tea ceremonies/candent light

The man I loved has become a moth

ଔ

Rigrag of mid-day   curls into slumber   Tomato worms
gather   static lightning   bouquets of statice

The years elide
on the tarmac

ଔ

Bone china: "Imagine the fire/that made this cup
shine/like milk, flower/blue as iron"

Marzipan, honey   beet fields under a nimbus sky

Persimmons   tart on the tongue/   rat's cry /
the eyes of owls   open into my sleep

ଔ

Apple-bells ringing from all the orchards/   only
the rind of the day is left

She is named Ileana, Irini, Illa   I, I, I

A cabbage moon is pulling the tides

CR

Her perfume is *Datura*

Some nights there is fog

_____

The quoted lines are from a poem entitled "Bone China"
by Theodore Worozbyt, Jr., in *Southern Poetry Review*,
Volume XXXIII, No. 1, Spring 1993.

Imbolc

Beyond the far infrared, microwaves heat our coffee. St. Brigid's day opens. Feast of the Goddess Bride.

The moon begins to turn its hidden aspects toward remembrance. What will we do when the dark side of the moon is suddenly exposed?

To remember mattock, froe, drawknife.

Caffeine.   Moves the aura upward, forward.

Evidence of the shift in focus from the external third dimension to the internal fourth dimension.

To remember horseshoe, post-hole digger, crosscut saw.

A dimension is a structure

                    Trust the meaning of asymmetry.

Month of Rowan: Is the willow beyond the fence already turning green? Only the potted kalanchoe's rosy glow.

                    used to focus discrete consciousness

A Venn diagram uses circles to represent an operation in set theory.

Fifty years after her death, Marie Curie's cookbooks were still radioactive.

Bees can see beyond the blue horizon. Beyond the red horizon, microwaves heat our coffee, radio waves bring political noise.

                    Position of the circles indicates.

Page From a Book of Hours

18th of February

the milk-blue
of early evening

hyacinths
in milk-blue flower

reading Colin Wilson's *Mysteries*

thinking of Time
wrapping around itself

the Future already
created in the Past

Easter Morning

the world no longer clogged with sorrow and ice
light rose like a bee coming out of a rose

the stars and Venus followed us home
the wind was pushing its scented broom

church bells rang

we wanted to meet him
the Jesus of lilacs and pomegranate wine

COUNTERPOINT

Bright sills. Enormous moon.
It is easy to think *wisteria.*

Do you smell the wood smoke in the air?
It is the smell of the Midi.

Slowly the poles drift
and the moon rides farther north.

Pink smoke-puffs fall from the mimosa.
A single blossom says *commence.*

ARTHUR MEANS *BEAR* IN BRYTHONIC

language, mixture of Celtic and Latin   start writing, she says, and
we do   new hardcover books in the store   novels   poems   where
are the books on cats, parrots, people from the Himalayas   where
are the green trees bursting   *a string of rosary beads*   into flower
catalpa   honey locust   words like *river, buckbean, moon*   when we
are gone from this place, who will remember us   who will know we
were here   when this busy street was a dirt road   when the nursery
offered gazing globes   snowball (viburnum)   blue gazing globes and
red   and forsythia   (there was lilac too)   but where would i go
to find a persimmon tree   do rabbits still play under the gooseberry
bush   where are the foxes of winter dawns   where are you now,
little girl who was my partner when we took the blackboard erasers
outside and beat them against a flat wide rock to remove the dust   i
want to remember your name   1946   amazing grace of memory
snows of *they say tomorrow will be* yesteryear   Jeanne d'Arc in
Rouen   it was May 1431   and this too is May   *come white* bean
pods on the catalpa   tree   bronze-green, the velvet bean pods of
wisteria   cargoes of light from the dogwood tree   cowbind that
dodders into bloom

was king arthur's name owain?   and where did

SYCAMORE

It is June. Sycamores cast their thick shade.
In Europe they are called plane trees.

Plane trees cast their thick shade. It is June.

Two women are reading about the death
of Raymond Carver. They are Americans.
They are in France. Leaves are falling from
the plane trees.

They are in Vence, where D. H. Lawrence died.

It is raining.

A scientist says he has discovered that water has memory.

What does the rain remember, falling on these
plane trees?

ECHOES OF WATER IN A MIRROR

1.   wavery glass
reflecting
crackled light
on a beach in Spain

a child running
down to the sea
crying
Voilà la mer!
small shells
tight in her hand

the sea
green at the edges
serene

the world gone mad
gone from view

2.   at Tarragona
on a bluff over the Mediterranean
a three-level villa
of honey-colored
native stone

"the pool halfway down
the bluff
can be pumped full
of either fresh water
or the crystal clear
water
of the sea"

3.   hold the shell to your ear
they told me

you'll hear the Atlantic
the way it sounds
just off Cape Henry

(in a supermarket freezer
in Arizona
Calmar squid
from the Virginia Capes)

Night in a Town on Boldcamp Mountain

The town floats
in lettuce-colored light.

Night falls:
 a lost moon drags the river
 searching for dreams.

Darkness hollows the doorways.
Young girls walk beside the river,
their soft shadows rising around them.
They hear low music
drifting like boats on the long water.

Cats prowl
through the reticent night
under the angular shadows of houses.

Daybreak:
 The foggy moon recedes.
 The dark lace of trees grows luminous.

And the seines of the moon
         dissolve.

ELSEWHERE

Summer

In a blue-painted room under the eaves. Dragonflies too
weak to fly in the heat. Flute music spirals upward.
Strawberries fall out of tin buckets.

> Jeux Floraux de Toulouse, summer festival
> in honor of the Virgin Mary. Poems to
> *Notre Dame des Fleurs*. First prize a golden
> violet. Then prizes of silver marigold and
> silver églantine.

World gray-green as rain begins to fall. What emerges
from the mist. Peach-leaves recall the key of C. World that
remembers rivers and Sunday afternoons. Tree-shadowed
rivers only.

Autumn

St. Emilion. Season of *La Vendange*. Virgo on the cusp of
Libra. A crumbling fountain under ancient trees. Odor of
burning vinestems. *It is very cold, this water. It has been
famous in this valley for a thousand years.*

Hay in the fields is brittle now with frost. A meadow
shining. In the darkness, everything a shadow of itself.
Grayness with a purple edge. Pine trees black as oboes.

Think of Flaubert's *Novembre*. But still the compass shows
true north.

All I Know is What I Know

*Vortex: A receiving station
             for direct influences*

mauve fruit
on the
prickly pear

brushfires
alive
in the
Catalinas

September
again

another
vortex

Tucson, September 1987

DANCING ALL NIGHT AT THE TRIBULATION CAFÉ

orange light - jukebox bubbles floating - the music always neon -
September stars - the Swan rides at the zenith - blues in the - bayou
night - cobalt blue - my momma done told me

in a South that never was - they would sit under a yellow-wood tree
and talk about the past - fascination of copperheads - rattlesnakes
- blowing vipers - what did you expect but tribulation -
huckleberry vines heavy with smoky fruit - black gum - shadbush

lion pit in the Circus Maximus - Deborah Kerr in a sky-blue dress -
Quo Vadis, Domine - nominative genitive dative accusative ablative
- caves deep in the woods - caves in Rome - on the south face of
Bitter Mountain

nouns of the first declension - air holding the sweetness of spring
grass - fully saturated primary blue - Deborah Kerr dressed always
in

working with neon is working with light - with electricity   fire
poured into glass - relation between *new* and *nine* - *nuevo nueve*

opera is haunted by the death of women - which always brings it to
a close - but *Quo Vadis* is not - Deborah Kerr does not die - dressed
in - with flowers in her hair when she is tied to the stake

stairs too steep to descend   - *Oh, Madame, vous avez le vertige*

dancing all night to Blue Moon of Kentucky - can one dance to that
song

summer has gone south - and taken the roses with it – and the
flowers of the plum tree

dancing all night
yellowwood tree - *honeycomb* - *tribulation*

SULFUR

color of light under November trees

always yellow   yet burns with a blue flame   no one is surprised
when crows appear in the south   *poisonous, yet a medicine*

pink is not a November color, though the pale cosmos stands
feathery leaves   pink-rayed flower heads

she enters a shop displaying herbs that resemble dried reptiles

letters of the alphabet form among the trees   the lower-case *q* has
no kern

native element   in England *sulphur*   burn in stale rooms to
purify

last fireflies of a plangent summer   amaranth candies
for the Day of the Dead

sometimes the color of tawny silk, of sunflowers

☙

a day after rain   cumulus clouds of astonishing whiteness appear
ash leaves float down   orange-winged sulfurs

does she believe in physics

liturgy of cottonwood, sweet acacia and Be Still Tree
of sulfurflower, wild rhubarb and red dock   gummy sap of the
camphor tree

❧

among these dragon flowers, who is to say what is plausible

sycamore leaves, forest of burnished sulfur

CITY INSIDE THE BLIZZARD

dark storm-beaten city of stone   pure lilting of electric flutes
gold spheres bright as glass   a radish leaf
nightfall   descent of snow and seeds

the moon enormous, dull and rufous
light shines from gold slits of windows

he came to this country   with opals and aventurine
to pay his way

do not think of him as man or woman
but as the four registers of voices

there are things that outweigh comfort

blossoming pear tree in spring snow   fields of snowgrass
groves of white trees   white leaves   no wind
and cairngorm shadows   at the mouths of caves

rain falling   the dust of summer   the city with its carbon heart
trees with pale-scarlet roots   zinc oboes playing

silver of rivers in the distance
ice rivers under frozen rain

the air is sullen as an old otter in a cage

he sang an unknown liturgy
and paid three opals   to have his future told

can one read a cat's face
deep bright eyes that do not change expression

starcarbon seething from the sun's white rim
she would not tell him   the day that he would die

what do you call it, this world

Notes Written in Purple Ink

April 16,1879. Bernadette of Lourdes is dying in Nevers. Orchards are in bloom, white petals floating down like snow.

March 13, 1917. Harvena Richter is born. She would become renowned for her knowledge of Virginia Woolf. Would know that Woolf ate from dishes of purple lusterware and wrote in purple ink.

1925. Guerlain's *Shalimar is* the first perfume to have vanilla as the dominant aroma—the "bold end note."

1939. Shulton's *Friendship's Garden.* Mingled scents of ylang-ylang, jasmine, honeysuckle, rose.

1952. High school Latin class. The voice of Julius Caesar ringing through the room: *Gallia est omnis divisa in partes tres.*

1954. Post-communion Collect for Quinquagesima. "That we who have received this heavenly food may by it be safeguarded from all adversities."

1956. The Virginia General Assembly votes to close any school that integrates. Governor Thomas Stanley and Senator Harry F. Byrd cite their "unyielding and massive resistance" to integration.

Harvena Richter, bound for home from Italy, books passage on the *Andrea Doria,* then changes her booking to another ship. Why, she does not know. On July 15, approaching the coast of Nantucket, Massachusetts, the *Andrea Doria* collides with the eastward-bound MS *Stockholm* of the Swedish American Line in what became one of history's most infamous maritime disasters.

Vocatus atque non vocatus Deus aderit. "Bidden or not bidden God is present." Carving above Carl Jung's door in Zurich.

2008. In the Vatican, instructions on the cash machines are in Latin. The only place in the world where this is so.

SOUTHERN CROSS

*"The Age of Aquarius is dawning,
and the world as we have known it
is coming to an end."*

1.

the night skies over Tennessee
a thicket of briary stars

her lovers have all gone south
lost on the freeways of Alabama
or gathering dewberries in Georgia

rain last night
in Macon and Savannah

off Bimini
the sound of Atlantis
slowly rising

2.

through dusk luminous as marmalade
Venus is coming in from the west

in El Paso
air traffic control
thinks she's the evening flight
from Phoenix

radios her
clearance to land

her approach will be
from the south

3.

in North Carolina
the flame azaleas are in bloom
though the end of the world
is coming

fat buds of roses crowd the trellis
nuzzle each other when night stirs

under the porch swing
a cricket *threeps* to the wind

in the Great Smokies
the flame azaleas are in bloom

and the viper's bugloss

though the end of the world
is soon

A Little Sweetness in the Noonday Light

The June day a perfect honeycomb. Air thick and gold as honey. On the tables at the Honeycomb Café, blue linens, vases of ginger lilies. Honeydew melon in green bowls.

On shelves and counters, jars of honey: clover, buckwheat, tupelo. Honey from meadows in Spain. Mayhaw jelly with port wine. Through them all the gold, radiant air pours the light of early summer.

Next to a long window is a piano shaded by potted palms. A man sits playing old songs, love songs from the twenties, the thirties, the forties. *Sweet, just like sugar candy. . . .*

Copper stairs lead up to a little room that overlooks a street shaded by plane trees (here called buttonwood trees) and lilac bushes. On the walls of this room, the gallery, photographs of bees, beehives, clover blossoms. Paintings of long fields of flowers visited by bees.

A dark-haired woman sits in the gallery drinking strawberry tea and reading a college yearbook called *The Beehive*.

A man comes in. He is tall and fair, his eyes are a dazzling blue. He looks at the woman. She looks at him. He sits down at the table across from her. She goes on turning the pages of the yearbook, smiling to herself now and then as she reads the autographs written by her classmates long ago. She knows the man is watching her. She tries not to look at him. He comes over to her table and asks to borrow the jar of honey she is using to sweeten her tea. She smiles and says, "Yes, of course."

"Thank you," the man says. Then, so softly she can hardly hear him, "You are so lovely."

Then he takes the honey and sits down at his table again. She pretends to be absorbed in her book of memories.

Piano music floats up from below. The pianist begins to sing,

> *He's sweet, just like sugar candy,*
> *And just like honey from a bee.*

She thinks of the words for honeymoon in various languages: *lune de miel, luna de miel, luna di miele.* Luna, luna. A town in New Mexico called Tres Lunas.

She remembers a river, morning spreading like honey across the water. She thinks of the river that flows through Tres Lunas.

After a little while she looks at her watch, then closes her yearbook and glances at the man. He is still watching her. She smiles, murmurs "Good-bye," and walks slowly down the copper stairs.

The song goes on.

> *Oh, I'm just wild about Harry,*
> *and Harry's wild about me.*

A week goes by. A hard rain ended an hour ago, but raindrops still bead on the lilacs.

The tall, fair man and a woman with honey-yellow hair walk into the Honeycomb Café. The dark woman walks in behind them, keeping a careful distance. She sees them climb the copper stairs, sit down at a table in a shadowy corner. She follows them and chooses a table under a southern window. She hears the woman talking, and sees the man listening.

The sun is bright now. Phoebe and mavis sing in the plane trees. Bees gather in the last, late lilac blooms.

The man steals glances at the dark woman. The woman with yellow hair tells him something about the hard rain that fell earlier that morning in the town of three moons.

The dark woman begins to look at an astronomy magazine. She tries to read about high summer on the moons of Neptune. She thinks the man's eyes are like the blue fires of distant planets.

His wife, she whispers to herself.

Grackles land in the buttonwood trees.

The same pianist is there, still singing.

Sweet, just like sugar candy. . .

In the silence after the music stops, only the soft voice of the woman with yellow hair.

INTERSTICES

It was a strange, mutilated April. The Cherry Pie flower
was in bloom, months earlier than was its custom.

ℭℜ

He had changed, that spring when the wool-mullein moon
floated above the Mobile River. Almost, almost, he was
able to tell her that he loved her, but finally he could not.

ℭℜ

Red roses bloomed on the wallpaper in the bedroom at
Oakleigh House. Blue paua shell rings in the shape of
stars and crescent moons for sale in the gift shop. The tour
guide spoke of summers long ago, when Yellow Fever took
a thousand lives.

ℭℜ

She thought of her life as a cup of electrum, alloy of gold
and silver.

ℭℜ

They were married in summer, when the Swan River
Everlasting was in bloom. In Alabama, in an old house
in Mobile.

ℭℜ

Where is the way out of this maze, through the fields of
sunflowers?

OPAL

though streets grow suddenly narrow
ponder larkspur and thyme

interrogate horses
grazing on sweetgrass

know there is wisdom
in cobra and copperhead

think of
cinnabar steps leading down
to a river in Wales

decadent moon's
silver glow
on the river Cam

wheatfields now
where Troy once was

praise
silver light on the burdock leaves
on the thistle and morning-glory

unravel
slipstitch of firewheel
and pearly everlasting

MARIGOLD

eclipse of the southern moon   the Mayan code not yet broken

flowers of Mexico in bloom

we who travel the starfields   there are many elsewheres

like a jewel was the green planet that exploded

we who sail on rafts of linear time   we who slumber

do not be lax in observing the stars

THE TOWN

Its Geography

No one knows where this town is. But travelers heading in its direction have been seen carrying *A Grammar of Spoken Brazilian Portuguese*. And there are stories of a great brazilwood tree that shades the public square. Other tales place the town far to the north, its mountaintops floating in snowlight.

Blue stars of the vinca plant smother the shade under the heaven trees, under the great brazil tree. Palms rattle their brittle fans.

An ocean laps at two sides of the town, but on four sides there is desert. Seagulls nest in the saguaros.

Its Moons

Some nights there are two moons, one black, one red. Sometimes they ride together, but often at midnight they are far apart, at opposite edges of the sky. Sometimes they are both full, but on most evenings one is a crescent, the other round as a cabbage. In summer they both turn gold.

Wild weeds grow under their light: cocksfoot, creeping bent, bindweed, sunspurge (here called moonspurge).

Its Houses

On leaf-shadowed streets sumptuous houses arise. Tigers loll on their long verandas.

On the bookshelves, scrolled legends from ninth-century Spain, computer printouts on greenbar paper from 1964, and books that won't be written until the twenty-second century.

On the tables, the soft tines of pure silver forks. In the handle of each piece of cutlery is embedded a precious or semi-precious stone. When they set the long tables for banquets (held under the gold moons of summer), the women put at each place a mixture of gems: an agate-adorned knife, a bloodstone fork, a sapphire spoon. Or an arrangement of diamond, opal, amethyst, ruby.

Poor people from villages in the desert or from the snowy country of the mountains are invited to these feasts. They are each given a piece of silver flatware holding a diamond or a ruby, or whatever stone they choose, in its handle, after which they go away to build their own sumptuous houses and begin giving banquets under the gold moons. Or they sail away in boats heaped with flowers to spread the legends of this town on distant continents.

THE WORLD SEEN THROUGH BROKEN GLASS

It is Tuesday in the Mirror World.
The notion of elsewhere.
The notion of glass.

The axioms of causality are being shaken
to their foundations. To return to the hexagram itself.
The *I Ching* insists upon self-knowledge throughout.

Does French glass reflect the pale light of springtime in
Antibes, landscape of *plein air* and perpetual ennui?
Will local glass reflect Antibes more authentically
than glass imported from another continent?

Virginia, 1942. Sewell Beverly was the editor of
The Dickenson County Herald. He could remember
summers before the blight that killed the chestnut trees.

Walk barefooted; there is no glass.

Hexagram 32. Duration is a state whose movement is not worn
down by hindrances.

Did Jim Morrison break through the doors of perception?
The smallest part can be a doorway to the whole.
Li Po pulled away from society to connect with peach blossoms.

Photinia (the spell checker asks if I mean *photon*) serene under
the honey locust. Pear leaves blood purple. Catalpa leaves green
hearts.

Is the world seen through broken glass *whole* or is it *fractured?*

Did Morrison read the hexagrams?

1943, Dickenson County. Children went from door to door selling Rosebud salve and mottoes. "The pure in heart shall see God" in glitter on purple felt. Anna May carried a nickel under her tongue so she wouldn't lose it. Glitter on her hands. Barefooted, wading the creek. Careful not to walk on slivered glass.

Notes from the Fractal Cosmos

A Calendar of Fractals, Magnified

*The magnification study tries to exemplify
the concept of self-similarity as we magnify
one particular Julia set fractal to a magnification
of 169 quintillion.*

Flowers burst out
roses with fires at their centers
and at the center the same flowers
the same fire at the center
and at that center the same
again;
roses with fires
to infinity.

*Some regions within Mandelbrot sets are totally self-similar;
others produce deep wells of stability (black regions), and whirling
vortices.*

Blue on green
a red fire at the core

lightning yellow at the borning center
blue on a lake of red

and honeycomb

The Lake of Dreams is a Black Mirror

1954
high summer and

the Linwood campus
stretches out,
a meadow in all directions

In the Music building someone is practicing, practicing a Scarlatti
pastorale. Piano notes, yellow and gold, floating across the meadow.
Tonight the lightning bugs will come out and glint among the
branches of the wishing-trees.

Noon, and we sit listening to the instructor telling us of music in
the Middle Ages *sumer is icumen in* of music in 1782 *sing fa la la*
of music in 1901 and someone is playing Debussy and the moonlit
notes are cool, they float down from the second story of the Music
building out the long windows over the sun-hot meadow.

If there were Julia sets in those summer fields, we did not see them.

Now a train comes chuffing in and stops at the station by the river,
the river that runs north. *Second oldest river in the world, though
we do not know that.* Bees hum in the clover fields.   Dragonflies
shimmer blue and green above the water.

1955 and *River of No Return* is playing at the Linwood Theater
downtown and Marilyn Monroe has only seven years left, but
Robert Mitchum has longer. And John Fitzgerald Kennedy and
Jacqueline Lee Bouvier have been married two years though
we don't know of them, don't know they will burst like crystal
constellations into our world, too perfect to be true. But everything
seemed true then.

A July evening, full of wistfulness, the sky above Virginia wide
and scintillant with early stars. We are at a dance at Squires Hall.
The band plays on and on, the old sad songs like "Tenderly" and
"Smoke Gets in Your Eyes" and the vocalist sounds like June
Christy. We want to talk with her at intermission but we can't,
because our skin is white and hers is not. Jo Lynn goes up and talks

with her anyway and for the next month is confined to campus for breaking the rules about mixing with Negroes.

Spring of 1956 and Jo Lynn is pregnant by Jack Hollis and he doesn't know it but offers her a diamond engagement ring that she refuses. She goes to Florida to find Ted Coleman and coax him out into an orange grove. In May, when the dogwood trees, the sarvis trees at Linwood are in bloom along the riverbank, she tells Ted that the child is his and in June they get married and move to England. She drives the red sports car Ted has bought for her, sends back photographs of the daughter he thinks is his. She does not seem to wonder whether Jack Hollis is angry or sad or hurt. She does not speak of him at all.

> *What was once an attraction to mathematics*
> *for the bipolar simplicity of correctness*
> *versus error has become a more profound*
> *appreciation for the juxtaposition of error and chaos*
> *within these mathematical forms.*

If there were Mandelbrot sets in the summer stars, we did not see them.

II. THE COLORS OF THE WORLD

Fourteen Ways of Looking at a Painting by Georgia O'Keeffe

1.

Thorn Apple, Devil's Trumpet, Jamestown Weed. Common names applied to *Datura stramonium* and related species of the Nightshade family.

2.

Jimsonweed: Tall annual herb found in pastures, roadsides, waste areas, and barnyards. Large, coarsely toothed, blunt-pointed leaves. In Mississippi, "Jimpsonweed."

3.

Conspicuous white or purplish trumpet-shaped flowers resembling petunias.

4.

Strangely narcotic, poisonous, hallucinogenic. Containing tropane alkaloids.

5.

A common sensation of people who consume tropane alkaloids is that of floating through the air.

6.

Jimsonweed brings its name from Jamestown, Virginia, where the plant was first observed in the New World. It derives from the mass poisoning of British soldiers sent to Jamestown in 1676 to quell the uprising known as Bacon's Rebellion. *"After consuming the black fruit of Jamestown weed, for eleven days we were in another world."* This according to Robert Beverley, historian of early Virginia.

7.

The large violet or white flowers stand erect and resemble morning glories. In late afternoon and evening they are visited by sphinx moths and hummingbirds.

8.

Jimsonweed, the literary magazine of Clinch Valley College, a division of the University of Virginia. *"Poems and art having to do with Jimsonweed are especially welcome."*

9.

"A Datura flower opened in my garden last night: a great showy bloom, white as moonlight."

> Andrew Weil
> *The Marriage of the Sun and Moon*

10.

Datura, of the nightshade family. Cousin to
> mandrake,
> belladonna,
> henbane.

All over the world it is a drug of poisoners, criminals, and black magicians.

11.

An old Zuni tradition tells of a boy and girl dwelling in the underworld who found a trail leading up to the world of light. They emerged wearing garlands of Datura flowers on their heads, permitting them to put people to sleep and make them see ghosts. The gods became alarmed and sent the boy and girl back to the world of darkness. But where they vanished, the same white blossoms that had adorned their hair sprang forth on a vine and soon spread across the far deserts and mesas.

Told by Marc Simmons in *Witchcraft of the Southwest*

12.

In Colombia there are Tree Daturas, almost always in flower with foot-long scarlet trumpets that give off a heady fragrance. Local brujos use them to induce altered states of consciousness. *"In this way we unravel the mysteries of the universe."*

13.

I dreamed I was in Colombia, in a grove of Tree Daturas.

14.

In New Mexico, at the corner of a busy street, a great Datura was blooming in the white delirium of noonday sun. In the sky, a Georgia O'Keeffe painting of white Jimsonweed hovered above the horizon, then floated away, toward South America.

In the Studio

Artist at the Computer

swirling lines and geometries paisley designs never-before-published images of Marilyn Monroe floral vector motifs stylized women against repeatable backgrounds *skew, shear, twist, and scale: vector images remain crisp and clear* look out the window and see Greek yarrow and moonbeam coreopsis remember too the red flowers of the chocolate vine when it rains watch wide agave leaves funnel rainwater to the roots

Artist at the Easel

abstract relationships of light and dark color, value and edge where reeds meet the water taller reeds on the left side accentuate the feeling of distance but what is the light's prevailing temperature take care that edges are not overly clarified additions of dusty violet-gray to thread sections together white and yellow wildflowers where the eye could linger final notes of texture

FLOWER

Rose in a distant, dreamlike garden.
Eglantine, wild sweetbriar,
        rambling the fields of Europe.

In this life she was born blind
and longed to see the color blue

Goosegog, Foxtail, Katydid

A celebration of the color green

color of numinous energies   color of the Ming Dynasty

absinthe   spearmint green   chintz green   Hollywood's
Zanuck green   celadon   celandine

gems of the green ray: emerald, aventurine, malachite,
green tourmaline   alexandrite, a greenish chrysoberyl
that appears red in artificial light

milkweed   mosses   stands of pines
fern groves   gardens   bindweed   rhubarb
goosegog   foxtail   rat-tail plantain

salamander, caterpillar, katydid, snake

names given to green paints: washed needles, cozumel,
bezique, tea leaf, arboretum, rainy day

Elizabeth Bishop's "drowned green," reseda   Stephen
King's "green smell of just-mown infield grass"

Poisonous emerald green in Manet's *Balcony,* increasing
the anxiety

Kandinsky: *green, coming together of eccentric yellow
and centripetal blue, expressive of calm and boredom*

Alexander Theroux: *color of more force and guises than are countable* Wallace Stevens saw green as reality. In Islam it is a sacred color. Priests wear green vestments in the season of hope. Borges slept in the greenish mist that is the world of the blind.

Note: Goosegog is an archaic word for gooseberry.

CANVAS

"One cannot be indifferent to blue."

landscape dense with chestnut and plane trees

skin of the river cobalt blue

first wind rises above the sycamores   a young fox swats
the boughs with a black paw   insects lift their claws and
rant   church bells ring out with diatonic ratios, occasional
accidentals   cornsilk stars bubble through green plasma

the model wears orange sandals with glitter on their straps

the air is filled with languorous music   she moves through
fields of oilseed rape, leaving a green trail

yellow pollen and blue-white musk in bloom   thickly
entangled branches and flowers make her movement
difficult

glyphs in Milk Hill

musical codes in the grain fields   luminescent orbs
dance in and out of existence, astonishing observers

the Moon is full now, for it is opposite the Sun

in atomic light, coherence is easily achieved

Names the Color of Rain

"Such an abundance of names for the infinitely nameless."

—Alice Attie

persimmon   pearblossom   dragonroot

algorithms of nightshade and
adder's tongue/trout lily/dog's tooth violet
blue-flowered alkanet/viper's bugloss

    deep-falling shadows of night, voice of green serpents

        catbrier
        devil's claw
        guelder rose

            names the color of water
            names that call out "night"
            names that speak the fear of reptiles

    calculus of rain and forests

hedgemaid, fairy candle, cat's claw, clover

pillows filled with the down of milkweed
o sleep o dreams that fly toward starlight

    dogwood, trailing arbutus
    hushed mornings of rain and flowers

pear tree sifts down
   its cinnabar leaves

Greece

a cottage
white as a sugarcube

geranium weather

ଓଃ

tomatoes
on their vines

a brilliant
scalded red

ଓଃ

house with a blue
door

spirits. . .

ଓଃ

stone steps
in the stonecrop
garden

ଉଚ

tide
trickling up

filling
the sand pools

ଉଚ

boats
pushing out

heading
for deep water

In a Pastel City Under the Pleiades

*"The Pleiades is a relatively young
cluster of bluish stars some 450
light-years distant."*

The house on Afternoon Street
vermilion dahlias
guarding the gates

blue doorways
and gardens of heliotrope
visited by bees

Flowers are ringing
through the rooms

Windows look out
on parchment mountains
on groves of
      Indian madder
      rough chaff tree
      ash-colored fleabane

At night
their silvered panes
gather the light
from young blue stars

Silver

In North Carolina, in the prison of her schizophrenia, Zelda dreams of a house under a sycamore tree, hollyhocks in the yard, and afternoon sun embedded in a silver teapot.

Summer of 1957. Full-page ad in *The New Yorker*. New silver pattern—a fork in Wallace's *Discovery* plunged into tawny sand. Was it designed by Raymond Loewy? No flowers, no swirls, only indentations that look like raindrops. Discontinued 1963. But on Atlanta's Peachtree Road, Beverly Bremer's Silver Shop carries it still, in this edgy summer in another century. "Inventory reflects silver priced at thirty-five dollars and fifty-eight cents per Troy ounce and public demand for casual lifestyle dining. Available now: Eight place knives, seven salad forks, one berry spoon."

In the art deco world of Agatha Christie's 1930s, everything is silk and pearl. Magnolia trees give off a silver light. Even the women seem made of silver.

THE HORSE OF THE DREAM

a white mare
    (snowlight
        no
           whiter)
waiting among
November cottonwoods

jingling
the
pearl-
white
bells on her bridle

lighter
than
milkweed

hooves
frost-
silver

mane
glittery
with opals

she will turn
and gallop away

into the
pea-pod green
of the sea

under milk-glass moons

stars
the color of
grapes

NEON

(Improvisation for a tenor saxophone)

already it is five o'clock   across the city yellow leaves are dropping
blues woman sings   her burnt
and smoky songs

banked fires at the field's edge
rainspill of blue vowels, seventh and fifth notes of the scale

fuchsia neon bends in rainlight   *diamonds cost so much*
because they contain galaxies

> ♪ The blue note is the vocal sound that floats
> ♪ between the major and the minor ♪

Enola Gay's pilot is eating ham and eggs at a table in the corner
fronds of silk trees feather down   chartreuse neon pours into
storm drains   *in the Diamond district, store owners undress*
the windows   jacaranda trees in purple blossom   ask him if
he regrets

"The more such notes, the meaner the blues"

℞

Neon, Kentucky is the last stop   a jukebox plays "Out Where
the Neon Lights are Bright"

pear, heart, oval, emerald, marquise

spotlit trees blaze in the lizard green   *diamanté dancing shoes*

viscous, translucent honey   violet sky against an iron railing
vapors and mysteries   who hasn't been that child,
watching the moon sail through clouds

women who will never own diamonds
are working the fields fully veiled

landscape dense with chestnut and plane trees
snow almost absent   cabbage leaves sparkle under ice

rainspill of orange neon

yet imagine a heaven of weeds

Wood Wind

Clarinet

spiroid notes, a galaxy
sound of chestnut bud and spinifex
(tempo) rubato   ><   stolen (time)
arpeggios the color of saffron

Oboe

texture of straw and gabardine
pick up stars that spill from the kettle
blackberry bush   deserted farm
night rain   catamount   mole
has a thing to say
says it strangely

Bassoon

immense sound of thunder breaking over stones

English Horn

asphodel
Isaac Newton reading in a field of moonwort
building a waterwheel in the stream

Flute

rubasse
mulberry
muscat

not wood but
quick-
silver

Piccolo

mercury of gold
honeybee

Recorder

a shadow-clock is telling the hours
Newton tends fires that burn all night
will he find philosophical mercury

Saxophone

chamisa   greater burnet   dog rose   strawberry
meadow-

sweet

FLOODLIGHT

early November   an orange
moon   a plane carrying
a cargo of perfumes

Elysium   Oscar   360°
Venezia   Summer in Provence

winsome pattern of villanelles
the porchlight coming on again
cargo of perfumes

Sirène   Gardenia Passion
Tribù

ଓଃ

"time
flows through prose
and around poetry"

New York   all-day rain
and Sunday morning sadness
winsome pattern of villanelles

ଓଃ

twofold light   backlit
untangling   branches of
a poem's dissonance   pecan trees

disconsolate   a sign
mildness   a signal
of its weather

                    ❧

              the woodthrush sings
              two contrasting notes
              simultaneously

"poetry is   the milky glare
almost   of coastal
silence"   light

full-spectrum   aubergine
light   casting   arbutus
violet shadows   dahlia purple

              the woodthrush sings
              two contrasting notes

ANGELUS

bee-stung hollyhocks   and sunflowers glistening gold

remembrance of
coal, clarain, and southern spatterdock

a street named Cinnabar
"oh, all the summers that have gone like smoke"

                    the color wheel spins and stops

                    charlock, sumac, strontium yellow
                            cobalt violet
                              alizarin
                                    tea-green

and cinnabar
"native red
mercuric sulfide"

anagrams of light   thrown silk

rainbirds that sing on riverbanks, in elder groves   not here

colors of rose: arbutus pink, rose dorée, rose caroline, madder rose
colors of blue: forget-me-not, squill blue, Diana

double-flowering Rose of Sharon under the eaves

sun-glade the bright
reflection of sunlight on an expanse of water

The Angelus is ringing in Vienne   *behold the handmaid*

red gazing-globe   cries
of new grackles in alfalfa fields
and bells that peal *l'avenir*

echoes of geologic time   *fissures that ramify through feldspars*

landscape of sand, cities whose streets announce
their stone and silvered names

and other minerals
adjacent to olivine crystals
that have been replaced by serpentines

morning rings like a clinkstone

     the sky   is starch blue

The Artist Longs to Emulate Wolf Kahn

to capture the way light coalesces around form
to paint canvases that glow like living jewels

    fuchsia ink of forests
    orange skies afire behind an aspen grove
    mauve air of pine woods

to record the green song of photosynthesis
the vibrato of yellow skies (a yellow like Van Gogh's)

to capture fog, haze, harsh winter light
to render old barns with agitated brushwork
to balance sensuous light with stark geometry

FROM A PAINTING OF THE ANNUNCIATION

On a green morning in the Mediterranean spring
Gabriel the Archangel, bearer of messages,
drifted through blossomy skies,
past islands of jade and parchment.

The woman stood by the doorway,
under a budding elder tree,
gathering herbs for the evening table:
fennel and dill and fenugreek.

Rubies crackled in the pavement;
the sun gave forth a purple light.

> *"Our Lady of the Rubies,*
> *Our Lady of the Elder Tree. . ."*

The herbs fell from her hands.

He gathered them up and offered them to her,
then floated upward, over the western gate,
his great gold wings beating the air.

The elder tree was in full flower. . .
and violet evening fell.

LES VERGERS EN FLEUR

Two Canvases by Van Gogh

Canvas 1

At the restaurant table, wine glasses upside down. Turmeric, ginkgo. Orange light. Enamored of starlings, grackles. Undergrowth. Point to Japanese models.   Chestnut tree in blossom.   Diagonal bracing. A cottage in Cordeville. *I am working in a grim rage.*   July in Chaponaval.   Unrest on the left side, picture composed in a classical manner.   Hills of Meudon on the horizon. *Now I am working on a field of poppies and alfalfa.* Journey to the South bears fruit. Return to Paris on foot, wearing a smock of blue zinc.

Space and objects do not correspond.

Canvas 2

In Arles and Saint-Rémy,
citron light at the foundations.
Economies of green. Cut back
the picture edges. Look into
the landscape through trees.
Tige d'amandier, brought
into blossom in a glass of
water. Souvenir de Mauve.
Brush strokes flicker. Not yet
wheatfield with crows, bruised
violet sky. Lower edges of
lightning.

Fringe of the void rising.

Intense Yellow of a Rising Sun: The Artist Emulates Van Gogh

"One may make a poem only by arranging colors. . . ."

— Vincent Van Gogh, letter to his sister Wilhelmien

glow of faint flowers in a dusky garden   frenzies of burning
yellows   transparent air of the Midi   not even the mistral
disturbs his brush   painting memories "that have a kind of
heartbreak in them"   close-ups of wild sedges and oat grass
spangled with wildflowers   hay fields in summer sun

must render intense color and not a gray harmony

oppositions of blue with burnished orange   colors that cause each
other to shine brilliantly   pine trees and dandelions   dahlias a
somber purple

blue cornflowers and myosotis   in the boxwood branches,
clematis and moonflower vines   foliage a burning, acid green

sun sheds a radiance of pure sulfur

BANK OF THE OISE AT AUVERS

(Van Gogh, 1890)

leafscape cool as rain
shallow boats like pea
shells clustered

light stirs the braided
leaves locust
leaf   willow
leaf   greening the
glassy shadows

a purple boat
arcs like a half-
moon on the
jewelled water

sandbank the slow
fire-yellow of a
firefly's under
side

a man with two
wives their hats
cool yellow
tea flowers

one boat
(with brittle
sail) red as water-
melon   the water
a quilted
mirror   glows
vermilion

LANDSCAPE WITH WOMAN WALKING
BESIDE A RIVER

(After Van Gogh's "Landscape with Couple Walking and Sickle Moon")

A warm day in a southern country.
Orange trees, jostled, give off their fragrance.

Flute music beneath the water,
a blossoming apple tree.

In the burning-glass of the rose garden,
a rowboat drifts.

> *You are gone,*
> *and all the flowers of the world*
> *are turning to lilies.*

Profusion of lilies. Water lilies painted
on mauve velvet.

> *Too many desires.*
> *We will meet again, and talk of red haw*
> *and swamproot.*

A night lit by comets, cobalt bells.
Cypresses/black flames licking the stars.

> *In the broken time behind*
> *this house I do not own,*
> *real orchards are in bloom.*

Rain grieves on the rooftops.
Rose trees are lifting their little hands.

In the depths of the night river,
the water bursts into flame.

> *That fording place on the river,*
> *where the plovers cry,*
> *when will your horse splash*
> *through its clear water,*
> *coming to meet me?*

I see myself in a red mirror; you are with me.
Twenty years from now I will look in that mirror
and see us together.

> Star flux in the highest darkness.
> Leaves are falling from trees in Guatemala.

Nothing will ever change.

K.M.

Poetry of night and rain, of absurd and
dangerous existences. Haunted by her
childhood self. Twofold remoteness of
distance and time gone by.

House on Tinakori Road, a garden party.
Karakas with gleaming leaves and yellow fruit.

Palette of a Post-Impressionist. Books on
white shelves fly up and down in scales of
color. Pink and lilac notes recur.

Flees the landscape of magpies
and foxes.
Searches for a villa in the south,
coo of the ring-dove.

Dismantle the scaffold of the story.
Precise effect. Capture the
shape of a salt
spoon. Rise and fall of every paragraph.
Match the exact music of a cello.

Van Gogh her writing teacher.
Language transparent glass.

Dreamt she was dead and walking in a
garden. Glow of cornflowers and myosotis.
Blue ringing against orange.

Roses so dark they turned black as they fell.

FIRST DAY OF SPRING

plum trees
break out in flower

pink as
>Mavis
>Maeve
>May

names I might have given
the daughter
I never had

If I Had a Daughter

What would I name her?

Not Elizabeth, surely.
    A venerable name, rippling across
        the centuries,
      but a white name...gray...no
        color at all.

Audrey?
Or Charlotte?
Names the warm
   color of cocoa.

Elaine, translucent...
green as leaves
in the first days of April.

Or Karen,
    the green
    of avocadoes under water.

Alice?
    The rose-pink
    of a rhubarb stalk.

Alyssa, white as alyssum?

No.
My child would cry out for a purple name:

    Laura, black-purple of grapes and plums;
    Julie, liquid violet.

Or Margaret,
    that perfect shade of light purple,
    a little darker than lilacs.

But what if she dreamed of a yellow name?

Then I would call her Andrea.

    Andrea, color of noonday.
      Color of the vase
      in Van Gogh's "Sunflowers."

ADVICE TO THE POET

Read the available light

Detect the presence of distant blossoms
Put contrast around the center of interest

Do not paint in fugitive colors

Remember that truth is rare
and dangerous as uranium

Do not succumb to moderate feelings

Summon delirious vowels,
consonants that glow, radioactive with power

III. HONEY LOCUST

MOON OF POPPING TREES

Moon of the First Snow

moon of ice
                snow moon

Moon of green silver
    etched in haze
        floating in frostfog

Red berries bleed
              under the snow
Red berries bleed
    in the heart of the world

while flowers wait
          in their icy stems

while flowers wait
          in unplanted seeds

Moon among the trees
    caught in the nets
        of frozen branches

the rime ice
    gives back your light

        Moon
           climbing the ice light
              toward morning

        while the moonvine sleeps
        in its moon-shaped seed

MEDITATION FOR THE EARTH

Earth Day, April 22, 1990

You give us raccoon,
        dense blazingstar,
        opal
        and apple;

        red passion flower,
        rapeseed,
        groundsel,
        jade.

You bless us with puma,
        news bee
        purple coneflower,

        honeybee,
        snail.

You gave us passenger pigeon,
        dusky seaside sparrow,

        vanished now,
        into some lost dreamtime of the cosmos.

You gave us (and give us still)
        bog spicebush, rare and threatened;

a plant called leafcup, found only on one mountain
        deep in Arkansas,

and whippoorwills,
        heard no more from porches,
          long summer evenings in Virginia.

Yet we rejoice, remembering
        spring field with dandelions, painted by Van Gogh,
            Wind River Mountain Range,
                    the musky odor of blue hyacinths,
                    the slithering grace of spotted snakes.

Earth, frail as a rose in hailstone weather,
accept our meditations for your healing.

Accept our thanks for
        a flood-scoured gorge on the Gauley River,

        the cry of loons,
        the dolphins' play,

        the boat-billed heron's cloudy wings.

New Mexico: Days and Nights
of Early Spring

ivory light in the sky

morning asleep
in its cold blue skin

୪

leguminous trees
mimosa   redbud   honey locust

Brook Benton singing "Rainy Night in Georgia"
while sugary snows keep falling

pale bean pods of the mimosa
tumbling
through updrafts of whirligig air

୪

Rose Monday: a sharp chill breeze

white bird eating black sunflower seeds

anniversary of my mother's birth:
hurricane weather on the coast of France

earthquake in Chile
shifts the earth's axis and shortens the day

At Sundown, Bosque del Apache Wildlife Refuge

how silver the wings
of the sandhill crane

in the last light
over the water

NORTH VALLEY SPRING

"Suddenly, so suddenly,
the plum tree is in flower."

Under the white
sweet-flowering tree

light lingers,
lost in radiance

IN THE MONTH OF WILLOW AND BLACKTHORN

white
plum
blossoms

in
salt
wind

April

moves
from Aries
into Taurus

and now
the redbud's

purple
purple

gives way
to
leaves

(not yet
deep summer

red with
rowan
berries)

Early April, Elm Trees Heavy With Chartreuse Flowers

1.

a morning in spring's
uneven weather

cold wind
washes the sunlight

in high
wind-rocked branches
of elms

green flowers
dazzle the air

2.

8 p.m.

starlight
washes the cloudbanks

driving home down Moon Street
I can see
plum trees flowering

in the night's radiance
they are luminous as snow

In Middle April

when redbuds/peachtrees/appletrees
are flowering
noonday rain
pools in the streets
a sweetness
falling
transparent spears
driving
through purple/rose/white
various
green

Last Thursday in April

a foot of
snow   will it
kill the
peach
crop   count
basie died
his
aprilsong
loud
on the 6
o'clock
news

ALL DAY THE WIND

"In May, when sea-winds pierced our solitudes. . ."

—*Ralph Waldo Emerson*

All day the wind
harries the mauve bells
of the foxglove.
They tremble
on their green stems.

All day the wind
churns in the treetops,
rattles the window panes.

New Mexico:
No sea-winds here.
Only a mist of dust
that turns
the rose-gold mountain
smoke gray.

BELTANE

"The Ohio valley is astir with May."

— *Merrill Gilfillan,* Burnt House to Pawpaw

month of Maia
goddess who greens the earth

in New Mexico
sproutkale month

blackthorn winter comes
and wind harasses
new leaves of redbud

elm coins rain down
germinate in mud-filled groves
under the pine and the flowering cherry

pink locust tree in flower
come, white sweet

&

in West Virginia
inscape of bloodroot and shonny haw

Upjohn and Lilly's chosen herbs
      mayapple root
      hulls of black walnut

queen of the meadow

༄

Beltane Eve
on the Tug Fork of the Big Sandy
spring peepers silver the air

the Tug Fork now an endangered river

༄

black warbler dead beside the water
sassafras lifting its mitten leaves

who can plead ignorance
of stars and lilacs?

JUNE

Spirea lolls in the hedgerows
pearls of snow
for a bride's bouquet

The world grows heavy
with rosebloom
and delight

HONEY LOCUST

subdued splendor
of the evening gardens

green silk of dew-lit grasses

cicadas
in the leaves of night

the sky unfolding
its skein of stars

ESCAPE TO TAOS

Come and write
>   *Where magpies chatter in the trees*
>   *and blind bees gather in the orange-glory flowers*

in Taos
New Mexico
>   *where houses fly away toward Cassiopeia and Orion*

One-bedroom
>   *(airs and voices in the summer woods*
>   *residual and enduring*

guest house
>   *illusion of moving water)*

wireless
>   *the blue floor of evening hovering.*

Internet
>   *Bell sounds and the cool*
>   *transparent notes of Ming Shu flowers.*

fireplace
>   *Nothing of permanence quite remains:*
>   *fire flicker, tremble of flame*

large *portal*
>   *everything in transition.*
>   *Why do we suddenly remember?*

grassy grounds
The age of memoir requires a memoir journal,

with apple trees   flower beds   sycamores
droll stories cutting through the world
like knives through butter.

JEMEZ SPRINGS, NEW MEXICO

morning

tall elms sift down
the paper pennies of old bloom
the paper coin of their seed

noon

in high
green branches
of the cottonwoods

angels touch down
dissolve

move on

sunset

light from the river
dazzles the flecked air

and stars crack open
in the poplar trees

night

shadowy water
water
watersound

all
night long

the lulling
river

LILAC

"Deep in their roots, all flowers keep the light."

— *Theodore Roethke*

green pores of April grass
bleeding nitrogen

bruised purple scent
riding in corners of wind

music of saxophone and bee
stone bells

the dark and the light
are never separate

Dark of the Moon

a dog's bark
backstitched the night

roses
were blooming

somewhere

Litha

Solstice: to stand still.

Solstice days. Lobelia gives off its cobalt light, its phosphors. In the town of childhood summers, the courthouse clock strikes 3:00. The long pages of afternoon, turning. White dog asleep under the cabbage rose. Topaz scent of honeysuckle.

In New Mexico, jimsonweed is feasting on plutonium, is thirsty for "pink water." Jimsonweed, of the nightshade family.

Solstice nights, aglow with noctilucent clouds.

Deadly nightshade.

NOTE: "Pink water" is the liquid left over from machining explosives that trigger atomic bombs.

Summer Morning

The wind rings pale bells
where wheat ripens
in fields the color of jade.

DIVISIONS

July 1
the air
emerald with leaves

today the year
splits down the middle

in afternoons
blurred with their singing
cicadas split
out of stiff shells

on the catalpa tree
beans
hang like green knives

apricots ripen
fall
splitting open

gold spheres
cleaving the air

LOCUST CRY

in the yellow light
of July noon

cicadas go wild
in the cottonwoods

hearing their music
I want to swim up
through the green water
of the branches

and sing with them

RAIN

July sun
glitters like a yellow ice cube,

Green radiance drowns the squash vines.

Wisteria broods
    in its brown thirst.

Xeriscape
    of beebalm and calamint;
    horehound, hyssop, mullein,
    and purple coneflower.

℣

The day moves out,
    reining a dark breeze
    that stirs the rose leaves.

At dusk,
    blood of mad rains in Embudo Channel.

In the drowned light after the water,
    the roses are quiet.

Arcturus rides in the thinning clouds.

℣

Now in Virginia
    rain on the kudzu and the pearly everlasting.

Black current of glimmering water,
Cats' eyes, chatoyant in the dark.

In Kyoto,

a leaf falls
from the hundred-branched
zelkova tree

and floats on the fish pond.

&

Far away, in some rainy meadow,
Thalia is blooming.

I dream its long-stalked basal leaves,
its panicles of bracted
purple flowers.

And somewhere a river flows,
black as leopard-flower seeds,
under the light of torches.

In sleep
I ride a long boat
on its onyx waters.

TICKSEED SUNFLOWER

Perennial in aridity and smoked light.
Rayed flowers exude bright yellow,
the color of communication. Black seeds
resembling ticks and chinch bugs, sprinkled
like peppercorns in fields and open places.

Leaves opposite (entire or lobed).
Craves sandy soil and July's crackled heat.

Blooms a long time, cut flowers in a cobalt vase.

HEDGE BINDWEED

le liseron   wild morning glory
a blue that stops the mind

flower of Montezuma's gardens   seeks
disturbed ground, prairies and wet meadows
hedge-bell, bearbind   clockwise entwines photinia,
piñon, pear   aggressor whose language is humility

blooms at daybreak in funnels of purple or magenta
flowers turn shy in noon's assertive light and close
at dark   this language the transience of life

Midsummer at Gilliam Court

flowing stream
under the leaf shade

in the phlox garden at noon
preoccupied bees

at dusk
a lone
faraway katydid

at steepest dark
glimmer of fireflies
over the water

ORCHARD, GROVE

hard rain in the afternoon

the most beautiful word
in the world
is *mulberry*

July Nights

1.

a wisp of wind
stirring the cottonwoods

melons ripening
like moons

2.

green moon
edging in
over the poplars

worms
digging freeways
under the sunflowers

August

noon

zinc music of traffic
on the boulevards

and paisley dahlias
catching fire

night

tree shadows
on the moon-bleached fields

are dark
and deep as wells

Along the Clinch River at Dungannon, Virginia

low fields
dream in the haze

milkweed, mullein
ripen in corners of dusk

an aluminum moon
rising

Dog Days

Summer steeps
in a brown wilt

But the cricket's song
is cool

It sounds
like fall rain

September, and Strawberry Leaves Redden Around the Edges

o summer
sweet
summer that
ebbs away
another

how sweetly you go
into old
quietness

what goat cries
rise
in the tamarack
grove

marigold
tansy
straw-
berry leaf

Evensong

September light is mulled wine. It is milkwood and honey.
It drifts down, down, from ever so high, from ever so far,
through the dream-pearled spaces.

It is glass and mulberry, rose quartz and diamond,
shadows of bees.

Peach leaves, rust-gold with dying.
And the late roses, berry-red,
that redden the shade-gray walls of the garden.

Beet leaf and squash vine. Sourwood and kale,
gone-to-seed vines
in the dirt patch.

Lettuce stalks climbing along the chimneys.

Night passing.
Moon at the edge of full; Orion floating.

Trees in a glass garden.

Mandolin weather.

September Villanelle

Now fall's first gold is in the summer leaves.
Bindweed unwinds in purple trumpet blooms;
September light glows amber through the trees.

No longer August with its drowsy bees;
The scent of autumn ripens in the rooms.
Now fall's first gold is in the summer leaves.

Through the cool darkness rides a satin breeze;
Soon comes the winter with its prickly glooms.
September light glows amber through the trees.

Drought-weary roses droop and take their ease,
As rain and thunder play their welcome tunes.
Now fall's first gold is in the summer leaves.

The sun sinks down into the western seas,
And southern stars are Virgo's limpid runes.
September light glows amber through the trees.

What do we do in seasons such as these?
We read the calendar of autumn's moons.
Now fall's first gold is in the summer leaves.
September light glows amber through the trees.

IN THE TIME OF YELLOW LEAVES

Reading "Sky Watch" in the Albuquerque Journal
as the seasons change

Venus turns retrograde
and locust leaves are woven gold

yellow appears in highest branches of the sycamores
the Moon is hooked on the claws of Scorpio

wind gathers slate clouds and fallen seedpods
a sparrow glints in the Rose of Sharon

right of the moon, the stars of Sagittarius
the North Star may stream aurorae

leaves shut down their factories
and xanthophylls emerge
in ash and poplar and catalpa

as darkness deepens, the Hunter's Moon
and meteors from Halley's Comet

scarlet and purple vines
a lyric that cuts the heart

Autumn

In the night world
of owls and foxes

the cool stars come out

and the moon
is a white rose

floating

BACH ON AN AUTUMN EVENING, A FOREST IN NEW MEXICO

Gilt songs of baroque angels
    above this streamy landscape

Oaks preening their twelve-lobed leaves,
    a sky lentiginous with stars

How the white moon dissolves, dissolves

Continuous Nuclear Reactions

October in Tennessee. On the Virtual Display
System, nuclear cargoes west of Memphis. A
constellation, moving. Red chard still growing
in the fields.

In the convoy, off-duty drivers sleep. Review
the manual on Use of Deadly Force. Light thick
and gold as honey.

☙

*Star: Any self-luminous celestial body having
continuous nuclear reactions that send out heat
and light.* The change to Standard Time reveals
a brilliant winter sky. Sirius rises, a blue glow
in the East Southeast.

Shooting stars at 3 a.m. River stones give off their
foxfire. The sun has found the Serpent Bearer.

☙

Consciousness is not stars symmetrically arranged,
but a luminous halo. Something real that shivers
on the far side of language.

CR

Stardust: A cluster of stars too distant to be seen separately with the naked eye. *An enchanting, dream-like state or mood.* Algol: eclipsing binary star in the constellation Perseus. ALGOL. ALGOrithmic Language. Hoarfrost on sorghum fields in Alabama.

Though it is winter, stars of the Summer Triangle are visible. Algol fades behind its dark companion.

In civil twilight, nuclear cargoes west of Tulsa.

Why I Wrote Out by Hand Ronald Johnson's *The Book of the Green Man* on an Autumn Evening in 1970

September. The equinox, dark coming early and a bronze rain falling.

> *of the seasons,*
> *seamless,*
> *a garland*
>
> *Solstice*
> *to equinox—days,*
>
> *come full circle*

I am at work, though it is evening. I am typing a briefing for the Air Force. Tomorrow the Colonel will take these words to Washington and offer them to Congress.

Carefully
the Colonel
writes down his litanies:

> the B-1 bomber,
> first strike,
> survivability

as if they were
prayers to the gods of war.

While he composes another page
I wait

and copy Johnson's litanies
to other gods

his songs of vegetable gold,
of white light
opening like flowers—
dog-violet, asphodel & celandine

a Celtic goddess clad in broom and oak-flowers,
and the Green Man of Wales
at whose command birds sang

ℂK

Because it is September,
because a bronze rain falls
upon the dark geometries of houses

Because the talk around me is of bombs and war

Because I want to *break out like fire and wax greene*

Because I want
white nights
when darkness gets up and walks

Because I want
moon-glade and phosphorescence,
and all things *rich and glittering and strange*

Because I want to think of rook and worm
only one cycle out of many
and bee
its dust & honies

of *dazzle* written in the poplar leaves

Because I want
to walk in gardens
gone into earth these hundred years

Because I want
to tell the Colonel
of foliage planted in our veins

to say to him
we stand in our rayed form

Because I want
to bring the poem into my body

to sing, note against note
its difficult
and radiant harmonies

All words in italics are quotations from *The Book of the Green Man*,
©1967 by Ronald Johnson.

November Evening, New Mexico

The year's eleventh lunation ends. The air, northern and melancholy, promising winter. The stillness of an autumn Sunday, sifting like shadowy rain through the suburbs.

Houses redolent of Mexico. Under the vigas, nostalgia of chrysanthemums, their odor like spice.

Slow rain of leaves from the gold poplars. Amethyst light under the rose-trees.

Firelight. Memory of fires that lived in the stalks of sunflowers in the high, fervid noons of August. Prometheus, smuggling fire to Earth in a stalk of fennel.

Halley's comet will be visible tonight, the *Journal* promises.

North of the moon, dark owls are calling.

—Albuquerque, November 10, 1985

SANDIA NIGHT

the mountain gathers
its dark weathers

and a deep wind
stirs the darkness

Tulip Tree Standing in the North Fork
of the Powell River, Appalachia, Virginia

Sometimes a tree tells you more than can be read in books.

— *C. G. Jung*

Tulip tree: A tall, deciduous, eastern North American tree,
Liriodendron tulipifera, of the Magnolia family, having large
tulip-like green and orange flowers, aromatic twigs, and
yellowish, easily worked wood.

Stalwart amid broken rocks in the center of the river,
the restless and unforgiving river, carrying its dank
cargoes of mud and human trash.

Stunted and small, assaulted endlessly by winds and
stinging weathers. At the mercy of a waterfall that
shows no mercy.

Sometimes a log washes against it, bending it double,
but when the log is gone it straightens and stands up again.

It cannot grow into its tall cone shape. It cannot open its
orange goblet-flowers, nor welcome birds to nest among
its branches. How lonely it seems, how mute and solitary,
under the glow of western sunsets, season after season.

When its sister trees along the riverbank break out in
fragrant tulip blooms, what does it whisper on the wind?

*(With thanks to Howard E. Cummins for his article "A Tree Grows
in Appalachia" in the Big Stone Gap, Virginia Post.)*

Solstice

At the New Moon of December, 1995

November gone,
its marigold light,
and plane trees bleeding fire;

Stalks of dead sunflowers stand,
brown ghosts amid the smoke of twilights.

December now. Bright stars are visible.
The abacus of days counts down;
the Oak Moon wanes.

Button seeds hang
from the bare twigs of sycamores.

Red skies at sundown, and the blue
snow-wind of bitter mornings. Early dark;
lights blooming in the Christmas trees.

We dream, like Horace, of gardens
and springs of ever-flowing water.

We long for flowers, bees;
for soft spring air
to stir the wind vanes.

Wan sun of Solstice noon
casts its pale promise
of the lengthening days.

Now, in remembered woodlands,
witch hazel waits to bloom,
to open its four
bright-yellow petals.

DECEMBER NOON

Blue, the limitless sky.

Sky that contains the galaxies.
Sky that shelters
the visible stars
and their dark companions.

Rust-red, the tips of leafless twigs
that carry
the vein of summer in their stillness.

Black crows
meet in the winter branches,
making no sound.

Pale sun on tufts of bunchgrass,
on the ghost-stalks of summer weeds,
on the jade green
of iris leaves.

Shadow where snow
lingers in patches.

Cold light that sings
from blue
branches of the spruce tree.

IV. SUMMONING

GERANIUMS

that tremble in the wind   beds of fuchsia   and red hot
pokers   hedges of escallonia in watery light   are
these ever to be found again

write *prosepoem tanka villanelle haiku*   buy
cherry sherbet swirled with orange *pantoum   tercet*
watch the little doves descending   flying down from
high branches of the sycamore

the smoky blue of twilight clouds turns now to apricot
and then to gray   *all you need is*   above the twiggy
 trees   *a clear view of the southern sky*

far off a bell   incense of Evensong   the hush of
morning   the morning when angel song and river light
and speckled stars were being born

surrender yourself to the summers and winters of your
childhood

A Season

spring of the wood-
louse
and
the worm

parsnip light

and voices rising
out of the long ago

WAITING FOR RAIN

"And sweet it is to throw the past away"

    – 10ᵗʰ century Chinese saying

Fragrance of spearmint
on the breeze.

Reading old journals.

The griefs of yesteryear
turning to candle-fire

to ash
    and rosebloom.

WHERE THE FAIRGROUND WAS IN 1948

there
where a ghostly Ferris Wheel
still turns
turns

where bright horses
of the merry-go-round
still
      rise
            fall
      rise
            fall

where the gypsy told me
my life would be

      long
            long

Toward the Blue Rooms of What We Remember

Ovum. Penumbra, density.
Illumination. A door that opens
into the rooms of memory.

Owlsong and lullaby. Soon we go
clothed in nainsook, nankeen.
Alphabet of leaves, music of triangles,
white flower of peppergrass.

Follow a mist into gleed and firefall,
sawtooth mountains. Larkspur and pearl,
mad flower of jimsonweed,
equinoctial storms.

The floodplain recedes. Cohosh
takes root in aquifer. Bees pull honey
from corymbs of yarrow.

Rose-papered walls, odor of chervil.
A woman speaks an archaic word, *gloaming*.
Dusklight, firefly, lacewing, snake.

Follow a map into remanent water.

FORSYTHIA

*"For we are the ghostly dogs of memory.
We follow a pathway
hung with the moments of our lives."*

—*Robert J. Levy*

March days with their fricative energy fields. *The long years
gliding as on a river.*

Forsythia blooming in bells. A scalded, ringing yellow.
Remember the blue, electric nights.

White froth of pear blossoms. *Remember
the diamond silk of your skin when you were twenty.*

Green sting of willow leaves. A wren harps in the cactus grove.
What does she blame us for? What does she know?

Write your life in obsidian ink.

☙

First day of spring, a cold wind leaching the sun's gold.
A black rain falling after midnight. Where?

In Arles, above the café, the emery stars burst open.
Sirius blooms, a crackling yellow-blue.

White almond flower. *Tige d'amandier en fleur.*
Landscape with couple walking and sickle moon.

156   Jeanne Shannon

CR

To go *back to one's roots is to go down to darkness*
Immense odor of pink hyacinths
so that the light can shine again.
Forsythia branches dripping gold
Learn to read glyphs written in the cornfields.
The air's drawn blue, the blue of Nîmes

Florida Coast, 1955

We smelled the slanting sweetness
   of thin noon rain on saw-grass

We drifted through watered light
   seeking the still world
   at the sand's edge

And built our campfires
   on the brink of the green Atlantic.

We slept
far from the bright afternoon
and the cries of the bangle-sellers.

In our dreams:
pink-roofed houses,

       slender moons,
        drifting,
          fading.

       And harps
    on the floor of the sea.

COUNTING THE STARS OF TEN THOUSAND YEARS AGO

cows in a field of red sedge near the milk gap
fragments of summery light, though it is autumn
wagons moving among the goldthreads

lamps blinking on, doorknobs cold to the touch
time when Rhode Island Reds come home to their perches
October light failing and melancholy

mountain path, avenue lined with dead chestnut trees
three days of rain, Orion behind the cloud banks
first memory: a black and white cat

first memory: a black cat, swans, a river in Egypt

SHADOW

Music playing
under the pittosporum tree

Songs
that moved us

when we were young

SAN DIEGO SUMMER AFTERNOON, SONGS FROM THE FORTIES PLAYING

always
    the old songs
    of love
    and longing

wistful
    above these
    streets with
    mineral names

           garnet
           emerald
           feldspar

the celadon waters
    lapping

Carolina Allspice

Sweet shrub, bubby bush.

A spring morning in seventh grade.
Easter Irene has brought a bubby to school,
squeezes it between her thumb and fingers,
till her whole hand is fragrant.

Tucks it inside her math book.

Even the square roots
smell sweet.

Summoning

There's nobody here from the long ago.
It's summer, and I'm alone in the apple orchard.

The Starks are ripe, and the Roman Beauties,
but no one comes
to gather the rosy windfall.

I look out through the leaves and
the waist-high horseweed,
and see the old schoolyard,
where, after the chalk dust and paper of lessons,
we played London Bridge and Red Rover.

But no one arrives from those childhood mornings,
when all the world lay before us,
young, and dappled in April light,

the Northern Spy in first flower,
and playmates calling my name.

Calling, calling,

Red Rover, Red Rover,
come over, come over.

SONG FOR UNCLE EMERSON

October chill on the Blue Ridge; your wife outside,
gathering the last roses. You had wanted to leave before winter.
You were reading *The Roanoke Times*
when your soul told you, *Now*.

I never thought you would come back from the dead,
certainly not to see me, little child of your sad, wounded brother.
You had seen me so seldom. How could you know
I had longed to have you as my father?

In Portugal seven years later,
on an April night bright with planets,
I was asleep in an old hotel out in the countryside.
You entered my dream from a moon-soaked balcony.
With you my childhood came back, singing its plangent songs.

All night you spoke to me under emery stars above Lisbon.
You told me how you had watched and waited,
hoping my life could unfold in sunlight.

We were back again, summer of 1945, on that road
along a meander of Crane's Nest River,
riding to see Rita Hayworth dance in a movie.
On the car radio, Ginny Sims was singing her song to the troops.
You were telling me I should never stop dancing and singing.

You called me by my childhood name.
You called me *daughter*.

WHEN PANTHERS ROAMED IN THE BLUE RIDGE

They lived in an old house

with long porches   miles from town   A dirt road full of ruts

Woods thick with white oak and maple and hornbeam
    and rhododendron pink in the spring

They bought a phonograph   the Carter Family
and a radio   Lowell Thomas   news of the War

She got up every morning   long before daylight
built a fire in the cook stove

made hot cocoa   oatmeal   biscuit bread

then walked two miles
to ring the school bell at Osborne's Gap

Sometimes she'd hear a panther   its eerie cry
only a shadow away

the moon still up
        and a few stars

The morning the Big Snow came
my father rode horseback to bring her home

Busy with drills on long division
        she hadn't noticed   the snow already
        three feet deep

Evenings around the winter firelight   She tatted

crocheted   embroidered   made patchwork morning glories
and perfect 5-pointed   cut-paper stars

Summers they planted   broomcorn   bleeding-hearts
carrots and beets   Kentucky Wonder pole beans

In the Fall of the Year   Mason jars
glowed on the cellar shelves

        tomatoes red as sunrise   bread-and-butter pickles
            Concord grapes in their lake of juice

Their second house   spider-legs bloomed in the yard
horseapple trees along the creek bank

She cried   when the coal was strip-mined

Later, on her wall a plaque that read

        In recognition of 35 years
        of faithful service
        to the education of the children
        of the Commonwealth of Virginia. . .

            Maple Grove, Trace Fork, Bear Pen, Osborne's
            Gap, Camp Creek, Sullivan Branch

Past ninety then   alone in her room at the nursing home
she told me things

        "When you were born   there was snow on the ground
            The doctor's car got stuck   down at Pardee
            but he got there in time

It was just before daylight   the roosters
had started to crow

I knew you would be a girl

 I saw things I wanted to tell you
        but I never did."

SONGS

When I was young I played the piano.

And sang.

In Virginia.

Trains would glide in at mid-day. Into the station by the river. I could see them from the window of the room where I was singing.

Upstairs.

Below, the long fields of the campus in summer light. Haze over the Blue Ridge.

My voice teacher was Italian. His name was Nicolo.

Rain would fall in the afternoon.

Nicolo LoMascolo.

Professor.

Fifty years ago.

Nicolo LoMascolo is dead.

Tonight we will sing songs he taught us. Arias and art songs.

Where'er you walk
Cool gales shall fan the glade

He was blind when he died.

The macula.

Before we knew him he had been a prisoner in a concentration camp. But he never spoke of it.

Trees where you sit
Shall crowd into a shade

I did not know of that when he was my teacher.

When he taught me to sing in Italian.

And Latin. *Panis Angelicus.*

His wife was small and dark and beautiful. Received Holy Communion every Sunday. Her name was Victoria.

At St. Jude's. The church was across the street from our dormitory.

One winter Sunday the Host fell on the collar of her coat. Plaid.

Now the building is no longer a church. The steeple has been removed. But over the front door there is still the pattern of a cross in the brick.

I was baptized there.

An afternoon in March. 1954. The sun was bright. The air glittered. I was 18.

Fifty years ago.

The priest who baptized me was Father Benedict.

Pastor of St. Mary's Church in Blacksburg, Virginia.

Do students today wonder why there is a pattern of a cross in the brick?

Victoria died long ago. He married again.

All his children are still living.

Do any of them sing art songs and arias?

His second wife survived him.

On spring nights in St. Jude's Social Hall, I would dance with Newman Club boys from V.P.I. Virginia Polytechnic Institute.

Moonlight and V.P.I., Fred Waring wrote.

And autumn nights.

I was president of the Radford College Newman Club. Radford College, Woman's Division of V.P.I.

One of the girls in the Newman Club questioned. She could not believe.

Her name was Teresa.

She begged Father Benedict to help her believe. But he could not.

I danced with a boy named David. A graduate student. Engineering degree from M.I.T.

Southern girls are so soft, he said. Voices like silk, like velvet.

Massachusetts Institute of Technology.

Did he think of me as *Southern girl?*

The phone in the dormitory hall would ring. *For you,* they would say. *David.*

A half-century ago.

Teresa stopped going to Holy Communion.

Panis Angelicus
Fit panis hominum

The doctrine of Hell.

She could not accept.

Trains still glide in. The station by the river.

Holy Days of Obligation. Father Benedict would come from
Blacksburg to say Mass at St. Jude's.

December 8th, Feast of the Immaculate Conception.

Of Mary.

Not of Jesus.

Of Mary, *conceived without stain of Original Sin.*

Ave Maria, gratia plena

One summer Sunday at Mass I sang *Panis Angelicus.* Professor
LoMascolo my accompanist.

Now it is summer again.

The transit of Venus of 2004 has come and gone. Did Teresa see it?
And David? Through a telescope in Massachusetts?

In Virginia the fog did not lift that morning, when Venus was a
black dot crossing the sun's face.

8th of June.

Rain fell in the afternoon.

In the afternoon.

Cool gales shall fan the glade

White clover was in flower.

Did he marry a Southern girl?

He knew Southern etiquette: Walking in town with a girl, walk on the outside, between her and the flow of traffic.

Not many Yankee boys knew that, we thought.

Art songs and arias.

Hymns.

Haze on the Blue Ridge.

MEDITATION IN FEBRUARY

birds in the cedar tree
their salt voices
rubbing the morning backward

grass the color of straw
afternoon a long boat
moored in stillness

such journeys we have taken
together
and apart

when the last one ends
everything
will be restless and perfect
as the sea

CUMBERLAND

remembered landscapes are left in me

higher now   the mountain rises
over the lake   where
drowned mornings linger

     CR

monologues
of trains and cowbirds

if it could be restored

the path   wind riffling the sorghum field
music of merry-go-rounds
across steep darkness

     CR

lizard hiss
in the dry
 sand-
   grass

dead conjunctions
   we cannot find again

ॐ

silver in the mountain
up at the Rimrock
and yellow groundsel
under the alders

ॐ

if it could be
as it was
        when

CARRYING WATER IN A SIEVE

we are pulled pell-mell
into the dreamtime

a wide field
of gold-eyed grasses

the moon reflected
in mullioned windows
old music throbbing

Audrey Hepburn dead in Switzerland
her husbands and lovers gather

she was young when we were

caged parrots exclaim loudly
blue roofs under a cobalt sky
full of exploding planets

the cuckoo sings
calling in a voice unchanged
from the depths of the night river

and where is Gloria Grahame?

even her biography
gone from the shelves

zephyr lily
beach wormwood
and rose campion
bloom in an old city

who will think of us   when we too
are women of long ago?

PATTERNS

"We construct our worlds
out of memories."

What memories live on
in the names of old silver patterns

> Woodlily
> Greenbrier
> Damask Rose

Oh, green summers that fled away

> Old Mirror
> Rose Point
> Grande Baroque

Summers in Richmond under the stars

> Melrose
> Woodwind
> Joan of Arc

Where have they gone,
the girls who chose them?

Their voices come back,
Silver and lonely in the dusk.

Hazel Mountain

Coal trains rumble across the Clinch River in Virginia. Spring
nights in the Appalachians, rain falling and firedamp rising.

Brush Creek

evening jade and blue
in the dream light
under the alders

air smelling of celery
of willow leaves and rain

cloud light moving
around the edges of the woods

a frog sings
d above middle *c*
then *a*

Horton's Meadow

how softly rain falls
on the tawny broom sedge
after long winds and drifts of apple bloom

remember the odor of winter hyacinths
the Virgin of Sorrows high in her niche

and things returning to fable and myth
"that was the way it was then"

the saints in their vestments smudged with coal

Paw-Paw Hollow

alchemy of clover and mayweed
white smoke in the firebreaks

she came riding a chestnut mare
through tangle of clotbur and dog rose

silver dew on the greenbrier
on the quill weed and maypop

when the firedamp in the mine blew up
on a morning when everything vanished

Pavane

Pink light
under the new
hydrangea,
its green buds
swelling.

Jacqueline Kennedy
is dead

       ജ

It's Newport, 1947,
the night of the Debutante Ball.

Jackie is coming down the stairs,
arms raised,
exultant,
laughing.

She's Deb of the Year
in her 59-dollar, off-the-rack dress.
She's Destiny's darling.
She's the Queen of Summer,
the Queen of the Milky Way.

       ജ

Newport, September
1953.

I want,
more than anything in the world,
to be married to him.

       ജ

At the Embassy party,
a stunning woman,
another one of Jack's amours.

Jackie is nervous.
She's wearing her hair up.
Her hairpins keep falling out.

ᚑᚱ

1994,
the twenty-third
afternoon of May.

Across the Potomac,
cathedral bells
ring 64 times.

Birds are singing
from all the trees.

ᚑᚱ

A young woman says,

     I wasn't even born then,
     but I had to be here.

     She was a mystery.
     That whole era
     was a mystery.

     But this is the end
     of what happened to them.

This is the closing
of a door.

ભ

Sweet May sunlight
above the graves.

How different the weather was,
that lonesome Monday
in November.

ભ

Sun in Leo,
Moon in Aries.

Where has she gone,
the Queen of Summer,

with her Sun and Moon
in the signs of Fire?

Autumn, and Lady Day Singing "We May Never Meet Again"

". . .the only thing that can save anyone—intense and perfect longing."

—Clarissa Pinkola Estés

Summer has gone, and spring's marimbas
(oh, grapedust blossoms under the moon!)

October now, and petals of cinnabar
on the trees

Cold shadows under the rose-canes;
midnights burnished in blue woad

On shelves in dark cellars,
peaches becalmed in their Mason jars,
grapes asleep in their sea of juice

At noon, honey-gold of the honey locust;
the past is gelled in a bell of light

Old music moves us
to grieve for the might-have-been;
each moment enormous, and all we have

But what awaits us?
Will we sing in the stars over Machu Picchu?
Will we become the guardian angels of antelope?

Pour lithium into molten glass

Nothing can save us but perfect longing

EVENING

(After reading Borges on a morning in late summer)

In the distant seasons of his childhood, the days and nights were full of splendors. They shine now in his memory like flowering gardens.

Time moved more slowly then. Winters were endless. But after all, the Equinox came, under a wayfaring moon. The earth began to smell of spring, of willows with their first faint yellow-green. Frogs stirred and sang.

Remembering now, he thinks his life resembles a fugue and falling away, like fading notes from a guitar, strumming endlessly.

It is the time of evening when the earth seems on the verge of saying something in a language he cannot understand. Untranslatable music.

He has tried to imagine a world without memory, without time. A language without nouns. Full of adjectives that cannot be declined.

As the years pass, the burden of memory grows. Who could bear to remember it *all*?

Once he had hoped that the mystery of time might be revealed. Unanimous days that tangle and untangle. Will he find again the squandered hours?

His life, how fragile and how wondrous.

A river radiant with golden fish. A cane field in the early dusk. Smoke rings around the moon, foretelling rain.

In his dreams, blue tigers pacing on a long veranda. The gardens of hundred-gated Thebes.

At the end of time, he dares to think, all things will return to where they were. Burned books will be restored. The woman who loved him will come back.

At 5 o'clock on no particular afternoon.

In the Bois de Boulogne, August 1914

"On the eve of war, the false sense of security was alarming."

—*Pearl Adam, English journalist living in Paris*

At the Restaurant Armenonville
an orchestra played.

Girls in black frocks—
satin and silk and chiffon—
in shady hats
and velvet shoes

and young men in gray morning coats,
abundant ties

danced away
the sun-glimmered afternoon.

In the dust-laden air
bright voices and laughter.

Tea and small drinks with straws
appeared on the tables.
A faint breeze stirred in the trees.

Luxurious vehicles
murmured by

and landaulettes
crackled along the gravel.

The sun went down.
The Arc de Triomphe
rose through a golden haze.

Beyond it the Louvre
drowned in a bowl of twilight.

The orchestra
struck up a tango.

GOING BLIND IN APRIL

Along the brilliant street
in the unbending glare of noon
tall elms sift down
the paper pennies of old bloom
the paper coin of their seed.

Another month, the doctors say,
before the worm eats the last light.

He dreads the fall of dusk and sleep,
afraid that waking will be night.

He hears the crinkled sound
of elm coins falling
in eddying winds among the cars.

He knows
no coin now
can bribe the worm.

Gold summer comes, and cars
play their zinc music on the boulevards.

He longs for night
when light comes back,
and in long dreams he sees
the crayon colors of the traffic lights,
and paisley dahlias catching fire.

After That Morning

*"On the astral plane, she has reconstructed
the home she had on Earth."*

The house is solid as stone. It stands at the foot of the hill
that once was a pasture, where blackberry vines are
blossoming now, white flowers radiant as snow. Around it
the light is golden and green.

Beyond it, woods stretch away, deeper than mystery. In
their loamy darkness, the mayflower called trailing arbutus.

The porch swing still hangs on the shady back porch. Her
dog is sleeping beneath it. Foxes run through his astral
dreams.

She sees her rose-patterned wallpaper, brighter now than it
was the morning she left. The soft tines of her pure silver
forks that will never again need polishing. Her kerosene
lamps whose globes will never be smoky.

She will sit in the swing and look at the old pasture, watch
horses graze, see cows come down to the salt block.
Remember the names she gave them in childhood.

It will always be summer.

Through her bedroom window, sun-sparks on bottles of
Avon's long-ago fragrances: *Foxfire, Trailing Arbutus,
Everafter.*

SHE HAD A FARM IN AFRICA

rain falling, African rain
cool as starlight
on the leaves
on the white
coffee flowers

madonna lilies in deep water
blooming like opium

Stravinsky on the gramophone
and servant boys
singing their reedy songs

ନ

guns
the sound of crystal
shattering

his plane gone down
in thickets of red milkwood

he is dead
we buried him
in that sabulous landscape
under the breath of lions

ଔ

in Denmark
under the snows
I try to remember
the ruddy days of Africa
the carnivals

lions disturb my sleep
I live
at the salt edge of loneliness
writing stories to save myself

all night the moondogs howl
in thickets of red milkwood

I die of *malheurs passés*
closing a parenthesis

SINGING THE DUENDE

We take death to reach a star.

—Vincent Van Gogh

without the possibility of death, no duende
   far off the voices burn
         deep-song song that wounds
        winds through dark water
   music of horehound
    blooming in waste places

        CR

         duende in moments when
       Theresa of Avila stops a bull

    when Thérèse of Lisieux rides through Santa Fe
         in a coffin of jacaranda wood
           and silver gilt

          when music breaks
        through frangible water

        CR

no duende in dun, bedraggled January
its cold blue winds

petroleum flowers hold no songs

❧

At Chartres
light through the windows
is a burning wheel

Tear down the scaffold
so that light's duende can emerge

NOCTURN

(Nocturn is one of the three principal divisions of the Office of Matins)

First Meditation

Midnight, and fall of miniver snow. Boats glide on frozen rivers. The milky stars take cover; moonglade dissolves its hieroglyphs.

The resin of deep winter
is amber, honey, frost.

>Who has poured stars
>into this river ice?

>What angel of black quasars walked here,
>under the willows?

Second Meditation

The mavis is singing from the water wheel. She sings of May, walled cities and their ancient apple trees. Bees hum in groves of shyleaf buckwheat. In clanging cities, glass buildings catch the green moon's light. Ghosts of white hollyhocks are glimmering. Echo, echo.

Third Meditation

Remember old orchards and river gold. Remember the birds that nested in southern maples *no peace I find* how they sang *just an old sweet song* on summer nights in Georgia. How they sang of the lost years before the chestnut blight.

Now only the chinquapin, the snowball and the nutmeg flower.

A porch swing hangs empty in the shade.

Open carved gates into hanging gardens. *Listen, the bells.*
Remember the smoky globes of oil lamps, lights going off in
Arizona and Rhode Island. Antares has left the southern sky.

Whatever has been will be again

The resin of summer
is in the crimson thorn rose and viburnum

unaltered, ever-returning.

For Alice, Saying Goodbye

What gift shall I send
to your new address in the afterlife?

    Perhaps
    a basket of tiger lilies

    Or a wisp of bright music—
    that song we sang
    forty summers ago

    Or a garden
    of rose-quartz roses
    the color of your name

V. ETUDE: PRIME NUMBERS

Etude: Prime Numbers

Two.   snow lantern

Three.   *Chaos, Gaia, Eros*

Five.   stirred cluster of rubidium atoms

Seven.   Myth is the ark that carries us.

Eleven.   Earth breathes through earthquakes, volcanic
eruptions, rain. Dichroic glass reflects fuchsia.

Thirteen.   Nocturne in F# Minor. *Chimère noire.* Deserted
farm. Night rain. Mole, catamount, pine.

Seventeen. Room lit by roses. The Celtic tongue is a sword.
The Physics of Angels. Why not you?

Nineteen. To dream in blue vowels is to name the world.
How many shades of blue, Colette? Wisteria's
fallen stamens.

Twenty-three. March days with their fricative energy fields.
Twilight of the Clockwork God.   Study a pine
cone, a sunflower: Fibonacci numbers in the
spirals.

Twenty-nine. The laws of the universe may be habits of action.
Sheldrake's morphic resonance. "Runnels engraved
in the texture of space-time." *The Presence of the
Past.* Lindisfarne's ecology of consciousness.

Thirty-one. Electron capture detector. Three *doshas* instead
of four humors. One has to be a *bricoleur.* Make
non-fiction an art form, *Wessenkunst.* The Internet:
return of the astral plane into public space.

Thirty-seven. Shifting grounds, horizons that waiver. When Lacan was kicked out. Tremors. Male-dominant primate band. *Blue Jade from the Morning Star.* Are we still trapped in the Bardo? Kittens raised in a vertical environment can see nothing horizontal.

Forty-one. swan that does not sing because its mate has died arbutus flowers blue as a ring dove   warped bells the sparrow's plainsong   we swim through ice gather leaves of mulberry and southernwood   in some parallel reality we are dancing the tango

Forty-three. It seems reasonable to conclude that. White Planetary Wind. Is there a science of metaphysics? Kant's Critique of Pure Reason, ornate tracery of axioms. Calling in a voice unchanged, from the depths of the night river. When did the whole thing turn into. . .?

Forty-seven. fluorite topaz zircon   Colette: "At night the white sand lilies, closed by day, would be blue." Aquinas said angels have no mass or body. Chaos gave rise to Gaia. Ouranos grew from her like a willow branch. Photons have no mass or body. Self-generation of the cosmos.

Fifty-three. Fifty-one is not a prime number. Divide it by 3. Renaissance Perspectival Space, world of the three dimensions of the human eye. Aperspectivity, context of multiple spaces, times, points of view. Everything all at once. Divide it by 17. Cult of technocracy. "Skip the whole dissertation exercise and write a book." *Scattered Light.*

Fifty-nine. Cinnabar, native red mercuric sulfide. A brilliant, scalded red. Crystals hexagonal, rhombohedral.

From the Greek *kinabari*, the Arabic *zinjafr*. The pigment called vermilion. Hardness 2.5. Specific gravity 8.10. House on Cinnabar Avenue; in the yard white oleander a storm of blossoms and poisonous leaves. Royal Doulton's "Cinnabar" china [pattern not yet designed then, 1961] arrives from a probable future.

| Sixty-one. | March days arrive with their restless chartreuse winds. Forsythia blooming in bells, a cadmium yellow, ringing. *Remember the blue, electric nights.* White froth of pear blossoms. *Remember the diamond silk smoothness of your skin when you were twenty.* A wren harps in the cactus grove. What does she blame us for? What does she know? *Write your life in obsidian ink.* |

Sixty-seven.   First day of spring. Jade wind leaching the sun's gold. In Arles, above the café, the emery stars burst open. Sirius blooms, a crackling yellow-blue. White almond flower. *Tige d'amandier en fleur,* green sting of young willow leaves. Van Gogh's " Landscape with Couple Walking and Sickle Moon." *To go back to one's roots is to go down to darkness, so that the light can shine again.*

Seventy-one.   A spectacular twin-center *Moiré* pattern appeared in Avebury on July 22, following the announcement that U.S. scientists had broken the speed-of-light barrier in quantum physics tests. August 13 at Woodborough Hill, a *Sun Flower*: 22 spiraling circles of 13 "seeds," each swirling around the flattened center in a Fibonacci sequence. Three hundred feet in diameter. Marciniak's annual Sedona Seminar. The FDA has refused to mandate labeling of genetically engineered food ingredients.

Seventy-three.   Winter rain in Southern Chile. I write this in
                 November. Jupiter is the evening star. Odysseas
                 Elytis died in Greece on the last day of winter.
                 White hollyhocks. I am free to keep a notebook.
                 Thomas Merton: "For thirty-seven years I have
                 been writing my life instead of living it." And again,
                 "It is not necessary to write a book. Or anything
                 else. One may write or not write. Therefore one
                 may write."

Seventy-nine.   John David Ebert: "So now it would seem that
                 religion must catch up with science, for science
                 is already returning to its ground of origins in
                 myth." Mist-woven twilight of the clockwork God.
                 Merton told us a great loneliness is necessary. The
                 loons are on the lake. To begin with they are two.
                 They allow no others. . .distances, wind, water,
                 forests, the loneliness of the North. He wrote this
                 at Gethsemani. Our Lady of Solitude, pray for us.

Eighty-three.   Merton's diary: "We do not realize that the fields
                 and the trees have fought and still fight for their
                 respective places on this map – which, by natural
                 right, belong entirely to the trees. We do not
                 remember that these little clumps and groves are the
                 fifth column of the aboriginal forest that wants to
                 return." On July 23, 1956, he said Prime down by
                 the lake. *Thick woods of birch, pine, oak, and fir
                 trees – and a great loon diving in the water.*

Eighty-nine.   In the Ozarks and the Cumberlands, when the
                 screech owl calls at midnight, it warns of illness
                 or approaching death. Owl eyes, chatoyant in the
                 dark. Athena's totem. Bird that hunts by moonlight,
                 no light. Waxing and waning of the stars. Learn the
                 wisdom of constant change within certainty. Think

of rivers in the South, the Bellingrath Gardens at Mobile, old houses in Natchez and Charleston and Savannah, and little hidden streets in dusty towns, old women watering red cannas in the yards. Owl light of the clockwork gods.

Ninety-seven.   Through solitude evoke the Goddess. Blackberries glistening on their briary canes. Of the rose family. In West Virginia, Venus is a miner's lamp above coal-scarred valleys. "*Long before I learned to care about cities on the Nile, before I was told I had lived in Memphis in 6,000 B.C.E.*" Metcalf: "In our severely disjointed world, *bricolage* may be our most natural mode." Mary Anne Thacker gave a talk in high-school English class about her passion for ancient Egypt. *To go back to one's roots is to go down to darkness, so that the light can shine again.*

VI. OF THE HOURS, SEAMLESS

Of the Hours, Seamless

A Daybook, Spring 2002

Morning

Newsprint.

Larsen B ice shelf collapsed. Small icebergs and fragments. The size of Rhode Island. Agency predicted.

Transport officer accused of rape.

African rue with white five-petaled flowers, toxic to livestock, has invaded eleven counties.

Sky Watch: By 3 a.m., the stars of Summer 2002 rise in the eastern sky.

◌

Sunbright shimmer on dead branches.

Birds eating black-thistle seeds.

March 25. Monday of Holy Week.   *But it is winter upon Jerusalem.*

Not yet new leaves on the Judas tree.

Sky Watch: Naked-eye planets are lining up. Wait until May.

Letter, reread:

> *I could have done so much more with my life. Should have gone to college. Would have excelled I know. So much is a habit, just leaving the house for an office in the morning, year after year. It's a place to be. For so many years of my life. Sons and grandsons OK. I may renew my real estate license.*
>
> *I should write my life story. The uncles who molested me. College was a term used in awe. We all went to the Lutheran Church.*
>
> *Merry Christmas to you. As I turned slowly around, the year was gone.*

Catalog: *Ralph Stanley and the Clinch Mountain Boys Live at the Smithsonian.* "Maple on the Hill." Cassette or CD.

Phone off the hook   didn't they realize   5:30 a.m. in New Mexico

Books.

Strange Birds in the Tree of Heaven.   hardscrabble world of east Kentucky   transmuted through magic realism

Ava. Repetition, themes layered on themes. *Vermillion* spelled with two *l*'s.

Afternoon

In the mailbox, *The Dickenson Star*. Ralph Stanley on the front page. Used to play on top of the concession stand at the drive-in movie in Grundy, Lee Smith told *The Washington Post*. Now a Grammy.

Catalog: Set of six wine charms.

Shopping list: fusilli, pecans, butternut squash.

First flowers on the pear tree. White.

At his home on Sandy Ridge.

Phone ringing. Do you want to see *Dragonfly?*

Balsamic vinegar, a broom.

Letter:

> *I am happy for her success. I named some of the characters in her book and helped her with plots, but she hasn't said "Thank you." She'll be signing her book at The Bookmark next week. But I won't be there. She's so rich now, she's become a Republican.*

Green Jamaica ginger.

Letter:

> *I am struggling to keep going, but you probably know all about it.*

ॐ

Kate O'Brien's *The Last of Summer.* Fictive theater, argumentative magic. *The moral right of the author has been asserted.* It was, after all, the late summer of 1939. Threatened cities and wasted loves. She will remind them that the past is inescapable. Fracture between deep vocation and conformity.

Yew tree on the drive still blue in moonlight. The river as loud. World of green baize, mahogany, and caged canaries. Only the people are unprepared.

Shenandoah. December 2001, East Anglia. Snow falling on Norwich, city whose name was graven on Saxon coins. The editor visited Julian's anchory:

> She could keep a cat for company, but not a cow.

> She could have three windows and a garden.

> She could speak with visitors, even the dead.

Friday, the 3rd of May. 3:27 p.m. A meteor crosses New Mexico.

Evening

On RealPlayer1, Lydia Davis in Santa Fe. Translating Proust. *By Way of Swann's*. Discusses the difference between *aube* and *aurore*. First light, first color. Publisher insists on *The Way by Swann's*.

April 8, Feast of the Annunciation. A moveable feast in 2002, because the 25th of March fell in Holy Week. On Rose Monday.

October Sky again. Jim Morrison: *Film confers a kind of spurious eternity.*

Roads overgrown with warm green danger. Jerusalem gone mad with fevers of duality.

Memories told in first person. Every *I* is mythological.

C.D. Wright on the cover of *P&W*. Search for *The Battlefield Where the Moon Says I Love You*. A watershed, the southern *Paterson*. Out of print. She brought it back. Lost roads of Frank Stanford's life.

CR

It is not idea alone that flares

but the smell of rain.

Take a cluster of grapes and set out.

ॐ

Phone call:

> *He can see the white lines between lanes but can't remember
> what they're for. Filed bankruptcy. Diagnosis is dementia.
> He's allowed to keep his car.*

He hired me. November 1987. Job offer over the phone.

ॐ

Today everything is like sadness, like something about to end. What
to do with these soup bowls from 40 years ago? White flowers at
their centers.

Break the thin shroud of conventional language.

Don't sit around yammering about writing.

POETRY

> *the non-word*
> *stretched out*
> *between*
>
> *word and word*

—Hilde Domin

Open up the sensuous fields in language, find the pulse that answers your interpretive vision. The landscape hidden in words.

Proust's involuntary memory.

> *Literary works require from us, the readers, that we become comfortable with the directed ambiguity created by the writer, and that we uncover the imaginative refinements of the writer's vision of the world.*

> —Rainer Schulte

Hardly ever is the resonance of a word what I think it might be at a first reading.

Essence of mustard flower: *for a dark, depressing cloud that comes and goes for no known reason.*

Phone call:

> *They're taking him off life support. He was going to retire in two years. Bought that gorgeous expensive house. Just to please his wife, I think. Soon it will be summer. You say you had a dream about him?*

Thirty summers since I first met him.

By what light do we see in our Technicolor dreams?

Battlefield in the mailbox. Voices out of the bruised South. Whose lexicon I know.

Write when you have something to say.

❦ ❦ ❦

About the Author

Jeanne Shannon was born on a snowy morning on a farm in southwestern Virginia, "the heart of Appalachia," when the Sun was in Aquarius and the Moon was in Taurus. She has lived in the west (Arizona and New Mexico) for most of her adult life. She writes poems that she characterizes as paintings—often impressionistic, sometimes abstract. It's hard to find one that does not contain a reference to a member of the vegetable kingdom, be it tree, weed, or flower.

She is pleased to claim Robert Beverley, historian of early Virginia whose name appears in "Fourteen Ways of Looking at a Painting by Georgia O'Keeffe," as a maternal ancestor.

Colophon

The typefaces used in this book are
Sabon LT Std. (TrueType), Kozuka Gothic Pro (PostScript),
and Trajan Pro (PostScript). Book designer Stewart Warren
used several Adobe Creative Suite applications
including Photoshop and InDesign.

www.ingramcontent.com/pod-product-compliance
Lightning Source LLC
Chambersburg PA
CBHW031834090426
42741CB00005B/238